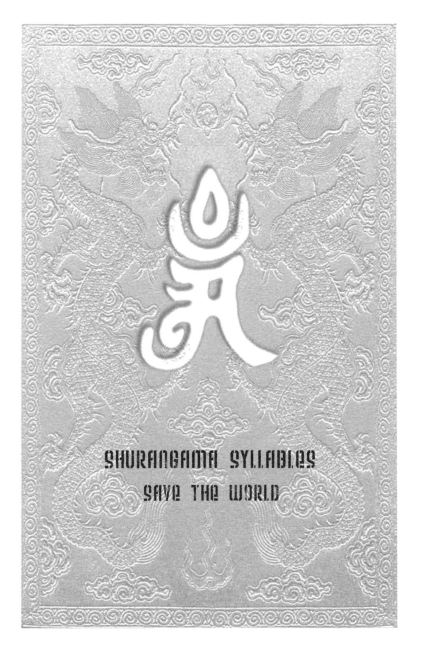

SHURANGAMA SYLLABLES
SAVE THE WORLD

Published and translated by the
Buddhist Text Translation Society

Buddhist Text Translation Society
Dharma Realm Buddhist University
Dharma Realm Buddhist Association
Burlingame, California U.S.A. 95482

Shurangama Syllables

Save the World

A Simple Explanation by

Venerable Master Hsuan Hua

Shurangama Syllables Save the World

Published and translated by:
    Buddhist Text Translation Society
    4951 Bodhi Way,
    Ukiah, CA 95482 USA

© 2007 Buddhist Text Translation Society
    Dharma Realm Buddhist University
    Dharma Realm Buddhist Association

First bilingual edition 2007
12 11 10 09 08 07   10 9 8 7 6 5 4 3 2 1

ISBN-10: 1-60103-007-X
ISBN-13: 9-781601-030078 (alk. paper)

Chinese talks translated by:
    Buddhist Text Translation Society

Compiled by Bhikshuni Jin Fu Shi
Translations by Bhikshuni Jin Gwang Shi, Heng Chih Shi
Edited by Bhikshuni Heng Chih shi
Editorial assistance by Elaine Ginn, Stephanie See
Certified by Bhikshunis Heng Chih Shi and Jin Fu Shi
Graphics, layout, and cover design by Bhikshuni Jin Syang Shi

Hsüan Hua, 1908-
 [Tian di ling wen jiu shi jie. English]
 Shurangama syllables save the world: a simple
explanation / by Hsuan Hua ; translated and published by
the Buddhist Text Translation Society ... [et. al]
   p. cm.
 ISBN 978-1-60103-007-8 (hard cover : alk. paper)
1. Tripitaka. Sutrapitaka. Surangamasamadhisutra--
   Criticism, interpretation, etc.
2. Buddhist mantras. I. Title.

BQ2127.T8722 2008
294.3'85--dc22

                                    2007017783

Printed in Malaysia
Note: Pinyin is used for the romanization of Chinese words,
       except for proper names which retain familiar romanizations.

I

Part One - Talks by Venerable Master Hsuan Hua

Part Two - Records of Miracles Related to the Shurangama Mantra

VI

Venerable Ananda's Vows

Venerable Master Hua's commentary on passage
from Shurangama Sutra

Namo Shurangama Assembly of Buddhas and Bodhisattvas
Namo means "to return my life" and "to respectfully submit." That means we take our body, mind, nature, and life and return them to the Buddhas. It means we are extremely reverent and respectful toward the Buddhas and make full prostrations before them. It signifies that we believe in Buddhas and we do not find it necessary to believe in anyone else.

Shurangama means "ultimately firm and solid in all respects." In all respects indicates that this firmness does not pertain to just one matter or one incident. This firmness makes us in all ways invincible and unable to be destroyed.

When Venerable Ananda became confused by a mantra formerly of the Brahma Heaven, Shakyamuni Buddha spoke the Shurangama Mantra. Then he sent Manjushri Bodhisattva to use the mantra to rescue his disciple Ananda and bring him back. Here, the Shurangama Assembly of Buddhas and Bodhisattvas is the assembly in which the Shurangama Mantra was first spoken.

Before we recite the Shurangama Mantra, we should return our lives to the Shurangama Assembly of Buddhas and Bodhisattvas by reciting this line three times.

O deep and wondrous dharani,
Unmoving Honored One,
Supreme Shurangama
Appears most rarely in the world.

What does deep and wondrous mean? **Wondrous** means inconceivable and ineffable. You cannot think about it. If you could think about, then you would know it and it could not be called wondrous. What is wondrous is beyond your expectations. Your thoughts cannot reach to it, and so it is called inconceivable. **Deep** means profundity. Not only is dharani wondrous, it is extraordinarily deep. It is extraordinarily inconceivable; it is wondrous and deep.

Dharani has the meaning of "uniting and holding." A dharani unites all dharmas and holds all meanings. Uniting means that all dharmas are included and maintained. Deep and wondrous refers to "the perfect fusion of the apparent and the hidden." Dharani means "universally responding in accord with conditions." That is, throughout space and the entire Dharma Realm, wherever a need arises, it will be met. No request will go unanswered.

Unmoving describes a substance that is eternally tranquil. Dharani is tranquil and unmoving yet penetrating everywhere. **Deep and wondrous, Dharani,** and **unmoving**—these three—are all deep and wondrous. The three are one. All three: deep and wondrous, Dharani, and unmoving are the dharani. The one is also three. And all three are unmoving. What is deep and wondrous is unmoving; Dharani is unmoving; and what does not move is, of course, unmoving. They are not three and they are not one. They are one and they are three. Each of these has its own meaning, but each can also be defined by the others. Thus, the three are one and the one is three. They are neither one nor three; they are both one and three.

Honored One, one of the titles of Buddhas, indicates that Buddhas are honored in the world and beyond. **Supreme Shurangama appears most rarely in the world.** This line praises the great Shurangama Samadhi. In cultivating this great King of Samadhis, we cultivate the supreme Shurangama, because this samadhi can bring forth all samadhis. There is no samadhi that does not arise from the Supreme Shurangama Samadhi, which appears most rarely in the world. It is rare. It is not easy to have this dharma be in the world. It is the most difficult dharma to encounter.

After Manjushri Bodhisattva used the Shurangama Mantra to rescue Venerable Ananda and bring him back, Ananda was grateful for Shakyamuni Buddha's deep kindness. To express his gratitude, he spoke this verse.

Extinguishing deluded thoughts
From countless kalpas past.
I needn't pass through eons
Till the Dharma body's gained.

Why do people have false knowledge and false views? Why are their knowledge and views deviant? Why do they persist with upside-down dream thinking? It is because from time without beginning we have been deluded. For billions of eons—countless kalpas—we keep having dream thinking. What are deluded thoughts? We take what is not eternal for what is. We take as non-existing that which exists and take what exists as being non-existent. We follow along with false states-of-being and are turned by them. We are incapable of not being moved by false states.

People are moved and turned by states. They do not try to control those states, they let the states control them. People are moved by the winds of karma. They may think slight mistakes are no big deal, but just because of those slight errors, they completely miss the everlasting true mind and fail to perceive its pure nature and bright substance. They totally miss the mark!

To be deluded is to think about things we shouldn't; to be greedy for what we should not crave; to be angry when anger is inappropriate; to let ourselves be confused when we know we should avoid confusion. That is upside-down dream thinking. To say it more clearly, our selfishness is deluded thinking. Not acting for the sake of others and only acting for our own sake alone is deluded thinking. Why can't we escape the cycle of birth and death? It is because we have deluded thoughts. We cultivate in order to put an end to these deluded thoughts. As Ananda put it, he wants to extinguish deluded thoughts from countless kalpas past.

I wish to now attain the Way
And as a Dharma King,
I'll then return to rescue beings
More than Ganges' sands.

This deep resolve I offer
To the myriad Buddhas' lands,

And thus endeavor to repay
The Buddhas' boundless grace.

Venerable Ananda says, **I wish to now attain the Way.** He's
making the vow first of all to become a Buddha. The Way refers
to the fruition of Buddhahood. **And as a Dharma King,** literally
an Honored King, meaning a Buddha, **I'll then return to rescue
beings more than Ganges' sands.** I am not becoming a Buddha
for myself, but in order to be a compassionate boat and navigate
myself back into the Saha world to teach beings who number as
sand grains in the Ganges River. I will rescue them all.

This deep resolve I offer is a kind of prajna wisdom **to the
myriad Buddhas' lands.** I will go to kshetras—lands numbering
as dust motes—to worlds in the ten directions. By the power of
my vow, I will return to lands numbering as dust motes in the ten
directions, **and thus endeavor to repay the Buddhas' boundless
grace**—the kindness shown me. I will, with extreme sincerity,
repay the Buddha for teaching me.

I now request the Bhagavan
To certify my quest:
To enter first the evil world
The five turbidities.

If yet a single being's
Not accomplished Buddhahood
Accordingly I also must
Renounce Nirvana's bliss.

I very humbly **request** the Buddha, the World Honored One, **to
certify my vow.** It is most difficult to save beings in the five turbid

evil worlds, but I still vow to do this. During the turbidity of time, the turbidity of views, the turbidity of afflictions, the turbidity of sentient beings, and the turbidity of life spans—**the evil world of five turbidities**—beings are extremely stubborn and hard to teach. But I will come here first and save them. I will first come back to the Saha world. **If** just one **being has not accomplished Buddhahood**, then, according to my vow, I won't advance as a sage—to fourth stage Arhatship—nor will I become a Buddha, or accept the Nirvana of Buddhas. **Accordingly I also must Renounce Nirvana's bliss.**

That is because as along as there are beings who haven't become Buddhas, I am going to stay here and wait for a chance to teach them. And, only after I have enabled them all to become Buddhas, will I enter Nirvana—attaining Buddhahood. The Nirvana of the Two Vehicles comes at fourth stage Arhatship; the Nirvana of Buddhas comes with the Unsurpassed Right and Equal Proper Enlightenment. Venerable Ananda wants to make this vow in order to help Shakyamuni Buddha teach and transform beings.

O great in courage, great in power,
Great Compassionate One
I pray would now uncover
And dispel my subt'lest doubts.

Great in courage describes a hero—a Buddha—as does great in wisdom, great in knowledge, great in practice, great in vows, and **great in power**. No power is stronger than that of a Buddha, a **Great Compassionate One**. Great courage and great power regulate great compassion. A Buddha's kindness can bring happiness to beings; his compassion can relieve beings' suffering. That is, everything is done in order to cherish beings, to protect them, and to fulfill their wishes. Whatever it is that beings want from the Buddha, he fulfills their wishes due to his great compassion.

Ananda asks the Buddha to **now uncover and dispel my subtlest doubts.** This is the second such reference. The first, when he spoke of **extinguishing deluded thoughts from countless kalpas past** pertained to getting rid of delusions involving views and delusions involving thoughts. Now, he wants to get rid of residual delusions—subtle as dust and sand. Delusions like dust and sand refer to finest submerged deluded thoughts, the kind we cannot even detect, going on in the most subtle level of consciousness—the level of fundamental ignorance.

Thus cause me quickly
To attain supreme enlightenment.
And sit within the Bodhimandas
Of the tenfold realms.

Cause me to hurry up and realize Buddhahood! I will establish Way-places in the worlds of the ten directions—places to propagate Buddhism. Someone is thinking: Venerable Ananda's vow seem quite contradictory. He just said, **If yet a single being's not accomplished Buddhahood, accordingly I also must renounce Nirvana's bliss** and now he wants to hurry up and become a Buddha and **sit within the Bodhimandas of the tenfold realms.** Doesn't that make his vow a contradiction?

No, it does not. Before, he said that he would enter into Nirvana only when all beings had become Buddhas. As long as they hadn't, he wouldn't become enlightened. But now, he is asking the Buddha to help him out, to aid him in getting rid of his coarse and subtle delusions so that he can hurry up and save beings and perfect his vow. And so he asks: **cause me quickly to attain supreme enlightenment.** Help me ascend to the highest awakening. He's asking the Buddha to help him save the sentient beings whom he is supposed to save. When he says **If yet a single being's not accomplished Buddhahood**, he is referring to beings with whom he has affinities—the multitude who join his Dharma Assemblies. He says he would save all beings who have affinities with him. Of course beings who don't have any affinities with him will have to wait for someone else to save them, otherwise, why would there be so many Buddhas? If Venerable Ananda could save everyone, then we wouldn't need any other Bodhisattvas at all. They would be out of jobs and would have to collect unemployment. Wouldn't that be so? Obviously, the meaning is that he will save those who have affinities with him, such as those who join his Dharma Assemblies and hear him speak sutras.

Now, I am not being Ananda's defense attorney. I really mean what I am saying. If all the beings in the world were going to be saved by Ananda, then what would all the other Bodhisattvas do that too? Would they just sit around all day and sniff incense? That would be ridiculous! Even the Buddhas and Bodhisattvas divide up their work and then do their own thing. In that, they are much like we at the City of Ten Thousand Buddhas who divide up the jobs that need to be done. Some prepare beds, some sweep floors, some rake leaves, some cut grass. We all work at our own tasks. It's the same idea.

You shouldn't think: Venerable Ananda has made a vow that is simply absurd. It is full of contradictions. By the time you are done with your criticisms, you depict Ananda as a common criminal! He started out making vows to save you and you end up indicting him! You accuse him of being illogical. Better that you watch to see that you are not being contradictory. Even if he is contradicting himself, it will suffice that you do not contradict yourself. Take care! Do not try to fathom with wisdom of a sage with the mind of an ordinary person. Put another way, a petty person cannot discern the thoughts of a superior person. To criticize people at random won't do. In that case, everything will not be okay.

And even could the nature
Of shunyata melt away
My vajra-like supreme resolve
Would still remain unmoved.

And even could the nature of shunyata melt away is expressing an impossibility. Shunyata refers to emptiness. Is it possible for emptiness to disappear? Could space cease to exist? Since emptiness is the absence of anything, could it disappear? There's nothing to disappear. But Venerable Ananda proposes the impossible: just suppose it could disappear. Basically emptiness cannot disappear because it is not there to begin with. But let's just suppose it could disappear. Ananda professes: Even if it could disappear, my vajra-like supreme resolve would still remain unmoved. **My vajra indestructible mind would not move.** By vajra seed of Bodhi, my great sea of vajra Bodhi seeds, won't change. Emptiness cannot disappear, but even if it could, my solid mind would not change. It will be here always and forever. It will never move; it will never change.

Namo eternally-abiding Buddhas of the ten directions.
Namo eternally-abiding Dharma of the ten directions.
Namo eternally-abiding Sangha of the ten directions.

This is taking refuge with the Triple Jewel. We take refuge with all the Buddhas of the ten directions; we take refuge with all Dharma spoken by all the Buddhas in the ten directions; we take refuge with the worthy sages of the Sangha of the ten directions. Worthy Sangha refers to all the great Arhats and Bodhisattvas.

Namo Shakyamuni Buddha.

Having taken refuge with the eternally-abiding Triple Jewel in the ten directions, we then take refuge with our teacher, Shakyamuni Buddha. Shakyamuni, his name in Sanskrit, translates as Capable of Humaneness and as Still and Silent. Being Capable of Humaneness refers to how he universally saves sentient beings. Being Still and Silent indicates that he is unmoving. Humaneness refers to his ability to respond and bestow kindness on beings. These two interpretations of his name represent the non-duality of movement and stillness. Capable of Humaneness represent movement; Still and Silent represents stillness. Stillness and movement are one substance; they are not dual. There is stillness in movement and movement in stillness. Movement does not hinder stillness; stillness does not hinder movement. Right within movement there is stillness; right within stillness there is movement. When we cultivate the Way to the point that movement and stillness are an identical Suchness, then we will no longer have deluded thoughts, for we will have returned to the oneness of substance.

Namo Supreme Shurangama of the Buddha's summit.

We take refuge with the Great Shurangama, the solid samadhi, at the invisible summit atop the crown of the Buddha's head.

Namo Guan Shi Yin Bodhisattva.
Namo Vajra Treasury Bodhisattva.

We take refuge with **Guan Yin Bodhisattva**. We take refuge with the eighty-four thousand **Vajra Treasury** King **Bodhisattvas**. Those who recite the Shurangama Mantra are constantly accompanied by eighty-four thousand Vajra King Bodhisattvas who surround and protect them. The fact that you have had the opportunity to find, to learn to recite, and to uphold the Shurangama Mantra indicates you have planted good roots, not just from one lifetime, but in uncountable billions and trillions of eons in the past. It means that you have planted good roots not just in the presence of one, two, three, or four Buddhas, but in the presence of uncountable billions and trillions of Buddhas. Now, you are able to hear the mantra being explained and still you quibble: Master, yesterday you said that for something to be wonderful, it must be that we do not understand it. So why are you going to explain the mantra for us? Well, if you prefer to ponder that kind of wonder, then plug up your ears and do not listen to the explanation. I will still explain the mantra, but you do not have to listen. You can just doze off and that will make it even more wonderful. You can enter the sleeping samadhi. You can fall asleep, start snoring, and go visit the Duke of Zhou. He will certainly say: Oh! Welcome, welcome. Glad to see you! He will then set up his chess board and you can join him in a game of chess. Meanwhile, the Shurangama Mantra will have been explained to its end and your chess game will have reached checkmate. You will wake up and say: What? Well, I don't know either.

At that time refers to before the Shurangama Mantra was spoken —several thousand years ago. The time the Mantra was spoken was several thousand years ago, but the time to listen to the Mantra is right now. Right now is not the past and it is not the future. The past is gone and the future has not come. You say: Now is now, is it not?

But the present does not stop. You say: This is the present. But it's already gone as you say it. Again, you say: This is the present. But that moment of your speaking is also already gone. So the present does not exist. Our past thought is already gone, our present thought does not remain, and our future thought has not yet come. These three aspects of thought can never be obtained. So what is there? There is the Shurangama Mantra. The Mantra is something that can be obtained. It is obtainable.

The World Honored One is honored in this world and beyond this world. No one is more honorable, no one is more supreme. The World Honored One, the Buddha, **from the flesh mound at the crown of his head released a hundred-jeweled light**. Buddhas have flesh cowls. We ordinary people do not have cowls atop our heads. This is a hallmark of Buddhas. From his cowl, the Buddha released a hundred-jeweled light **and a thousand-petalled rare lotus arose from the midst of the light**. The hundred jewels represent a hundred realms. The thousand petals represent the thousand Suchnesses. Suchness is beyond words. It is thus. There is nothing that can be said about it. In each of the hundred real there are Ten Suchnesses:
1. The Suchness of attributes;
2. The Suchness of the nature;
3. The Suchness of substance;
4. The Suchness of power;
5. The Suchness of deeds;
6. The Suchness of causes;
7. The Suchness of conditions;

8. The Suchness of results;

9. The Suchness of rewards/retributions;

10. The Suchness of original and ultimate equality.

There is nothing you can say about these. They are thus. You are thus; I am thus; we are mutually thus. There is nothing to be said. It is all thus and thus. So just close your mouth.

The hundred-jeweled light represents the hundred realms. The thousand-petalled precious lotus represents the thousand Suchnesses. Although we say it in this way, the equations are not as simple as that. This represents not merely a hundred realms and a thousand Suchnesses, but uncountable and unending, measureless and boundless things. It can be said that there's nothing in the three-fold great-thousand world system that is not emanating from the hundred-jeweled light and the thousand-petalled lotus atop the Buddha's crown.

Seated within the precious flower was a transformation body of the Thus Come One. Transformation occurs when something comes from nothing or when nothing becomes something. If you say a transformation is there, it isn't really there; but if you say it is not there, it seems to be! Suddenly it is there; suddenly it is not. When we perceive it is in front of us, suddenly it is behind us. That is how transformations are. You look all around for them, but you cannot find them.

From his **crown** that transformation Buddha **in turn emitted ten rays of the hundred-jeweled effulgence.** That transformation Buddha atop the crown of Shakyamuni Buddha's head emitted hundred-jeweled light that shone throughout the ten directions. The ten rays of light represent the Ten Dharma Realms. The hundred-jeweled light represents again the hundred realms.

All the myriad light shone 'round about, everywhere revealing secret trace vajra spirits, many as the sands of ten Ganges Rivers. These vajra Dharma protectors secretly guard us. We may not see them, but they are surely there. Those who uphold the Shurangama will have, at the very least, eighty-four thousand vajra spirits protecting them. Here, the reference is not just to eighty-four thousand, they are as many as sands in the Ganges' Rivers. How many sand grains does the Ganges River have? Uncountably many. Even a computer could not calculate how many.

Each holding aloft a mountain and wielding a pestle, they pervaded the realm of empty space. Can you imagine a mountain in one hand and a vajra pestle in the other? How powerful!

The great assembly gazed upward at once filled with fear and admiration. They peered upward with trepidation, timid as rabbits. They were awestruck, they could not bear to look! But they had to look, because they felt so much admiration. They were in a quandary: they couldn't bear to look, but they couldn't bear not to. They thought they wanted to look, but when they did, they were so awestruck that their hair stood on end.

Seeking the Buddha's kind protection, they single-mindedly listened, as, streaming light at the Buddha's invisible crown the transformation Thus Come One proclaimed the spiritual mantra. They were single-minded. That means they did not have any deluded thoughts. Females were not thinking of males and males were not thinking of females. They were focused and had no second thoughts. They were not like you who are thinking right now, Master, it is so cold here! Where I come from the climate is not so cold. On the one hand you appear to be listening, but on the other hand you are entertaining a lot of false thoughts.

Single-mindedly, those in the Great Assembly listened to the Thus Come One atop the invisible crown of Shakyamuni Buddha's head That invisible crown cannot be seen. The more they gazed upward, the higher it became. The more they wanted to probe it, the deeper it was. They seemed to perceive it in front of them, but then it suddenly was in back. The invisible crown is as if there and yet as if not. Although it is not there, it seems to be there. They could not see it and yet they also didn't see it—the transformation Buddha within the jeweled lotus emitting hundred-jeweled light from the invisible crown.

The Great Assembly single-mindedly listened as the transformation Thus Come One proclaimed the spiritual mantra. Shakyamuni Buddha's transformation Buddha spoke the mantra. Not everyone could hear it. The great Bodhisattvas could hear it. Perhaps in this scientific age everyone could hear it. However, if you want to hear it, you first have to study and practice the Shurangama Mantra. Once you have studied it well, then you can hear it

Mo he sa dan duo bo da la Dharani Mantra. That is the name of the Shurangama Mantra. It is also called **Light from the Buddha's Crown mo he sa dan duo bo da la (Mahasitatapatra) Foremost Spiritual Mantra.**

Mo he, a Sanskrit term, means great and points to the substance, the attributes, and the functions all being great. The substance pervades the ten directions and so it is called great. The functions pervade space to the ends of the Dharma Realm. The attributes have no attributes. What attributes could a mantra have? Although it has no attributes, there is nowhere its attributes are not displayed. Its function is that it does not have a function, yet there is no function it does not perform. Throughout space to the ends of the Dharma Realm, the function is a great function. That is the meaning of mo he.

Mo he describes **sa dan duo. Sa dan duo**, *sitata* in Sanskrit, translates as white. White has the meaning of pure and undefiled. When we refer to a Dharani as being pure white we mean there is nothing defiling in it. Attributes removed from any defilement are represented by the color white. Everyone should remember that the Shurangama Mantra is a pure white dharma.

Bo da la, *patra* in Sanskrit, translates as canopy. This canopy is an analogy for the mantra. The canopy functions to protect those with myriad virtues. Again, the function of the canopy is to protect and guard all those with virtue. Whoever has virtue will be able to encounter this pure white dharma. Those without virtue have no chance of meeting with this dharma.

I.

1) na mo sa dan tuo
2) su qie duo ye
3) e la he di
4) san miao san pu tuo xie
5) na mo sa dan tuo
6) fo tuo ju zhi shai ni shan
7) na mo sa po
8) bo tuo bo di
9) sa duo pi bi
10) na mo sa duo nan
11) san miao san pu tuo
12) ju zhi nan
13) suo she la po jia
14) seng qie nan
15) na mo lu ji e luo han duo nan
16) na mo su lu duo bo nuo nan
17) na mo suo jie li tuo qie mi nan
18) na mo lu ji san miao qie duo nan
19) san miao qie bo la
20) di bo duo nuo nan
21) na mo ti po li shai nan
22) na mo xi tuo ye
23) pi di ye
24) tuo la li shai nan
25) she bo nu
26) jie la he
27) suo he suo la mo tuo nan
28) na mo ba la he mo ni
29) na mo yin tuo la ye
30) na mo po qie po di
31) lu tuo la ye

32) wu mo bo di

33) suo xi ye ye

34) na mo po qie po di

35) nuo la ye

36) na ye

37) pan zhe mo he san mu tuo la

38) na mo xi jie li duo ye

39) na mo po qie po di

40) mo he jia la ye

41) di li bo la na

42) qie la pi tuo la

43) bo na jia la ye

44) e di mu di

45) shi mo she nuo ni

46) po xi ni

47) mo dan li qie na

48) na mo xi jie li duo ye

49) na mo po qie po di

50) duo tuo qie duo ju la ye

51) na mo bo tou mo ju la ye

52) na mo ba she la ju la ye

53) na mo mo ni ju la ye

54) na mo qie she ju la ye

55) na mo po qie po di

56) di li cha

57) shu la xi na

58) bo la he la na la she ye

59) duo tuo qie duo ye

60) na mo po qie po di

61) na mo e mi duo po ye

62) duo tuo qie duo ye

63) e la he di

64) san miao san pu tuo ye

65) na mo po qie po di

66) e chu pi ye

67) duo tuo qie duo ye

68) e la he di

69) san miao san pu tuo ye

70) na mo po qie po di

71) pi sha she ye

72) ju lu fei zhu li ye

73) bo la po la she ye

74) duo tuo qie duo ye

75) na mo po qie po di

76) san bu shi bi duo

77) sa lian nai la la she ye

78) duo tuo qie duo ye

79) e la he di

80) san miao san pu tuo ye

81) na mo po qie po di

82) she ji ye mu nuo ye

83) duo tuo qie duo ye

84) e la he di

85) san miao san pu tuo ye

86) na mo po qie po di

87) la dan na ji du la she ye

88) duo tuo qie duo ye

89) e la he di

90) san miao san pu tuo ye

91) di piao

92) na mo sa jie li duo

93) yi tan po qie po duo

94) sa dan tuo qie du shai ni shan

95) sa dan duo bo da lan

96) na mo e po la shi dan
97) bo la di
98) yang qi la
99) sa la po
100) bo duo jie la he
101) ni jie la he
102) jie jia la he ni
103) ba la bi di ye
104) chi tuo ni
105) e jia la
106) mi li zhu
107) bo li dan la ye
108) ning jie li
109) sa la po
110) pan tuo nuo
111) mu cha ni
112) sa la po
113) tu shai zha
114) tu xi fa
115) bo na ni
116) fa la ni
117) zhe du la
118) shi di nan
119) jie la he
120) suo he sa la ruo she
121) pi duo beng suo na jie li
122) e shai zha bing she di nan
123) na cha cha dan la ruo she
124) bo la sa tuo na jie li
125) e shai zha nan
126) mo he jie la he ruo she
127) pi duo beng sa na jie li

128) sa po she du lu

129) ni po la ruo she

130) hu lan tu xi fa

131) nan zhe na she ni

132) bi sha she

133) xi dan la

134) e ji ni

135) wu tuo jia la ruo she

136) e bo la shi duo ju la

137) mo he bo la zhan chi

138) mo he die duo

139) mo he di she

140) mo he shui duo she po la

141) mo he ba la pan tuo la

142) po xi ni

143) e li ye duo la

144) pi li ju zhi

145) shi po pi she ye

146) ba she la mo li di

147) pi she lu duo

148) bo teng wang jia

149) ba she la zhi he nuo e zhe

150) mo la zhi po

151) bo la zhi duo

152) ba she la shan chi

153) pi she la zhe

154) shan duo she

155) pi ti po

156) bu shi duo

157) su mo lu bo

158) mo he shui duo

159) e li ye duo la

160) mo he po la e bo la
161) ba she la shang jie la zhi po
162) ba she la ju mo li
163) ju lan tuo li
164) ba she la he sa duo zhe
165) pi di ye
166) qian zhe nuo
167) mo li jia
168) ku su mu
169) po jie la duo nuo
170) pi lu zhe na
171) ju li ye
172) ye la tu
173) shai ni shan
174) pi zhe lan po mo ni zhe
175) ba she la jia na jia bo la po
176) lu she na
177) ba she la dun zhi zhe
178) shui duo zhe
179) jia mo la
180) cha che shi
181) bo la po
182) yi di yi di
183) mu tuo la
184) jie na
185) suo pi la chan
186) jue fan du
187) yin tu na mo mo xie

II.

188) wu xin
189) li shai jie na
190) bo la she xi duo

191) sa dan tuo
192) qie du shai ni shan
193) hu xin du lu yong
194) zhan po na
195) hu xin du lu yong
196) xi dan po na
197) hu xin du lu yong
198) bo la shai di ye
199) san bo cha
200) na jie la
201) hu xin du lu yong
202) sa po yao cha
203) he la cha suo
204) jie la he ruo she
205) pi teng beng sa na jie la
206) hu xin du lu yong
207) zhe du la
208) shi di nan
209) jie la he
210) suo he sa la nan
211) pi teng beng sa na la
212) hu xin du lu yong
213) la cha
214) po qie fan
215) sa dan tuo
216) qie du shai ni shan
217) bo la dian
218) she ji li
219) mo he suo he sa la
220) bo shu suo he sa la
221) shi li sha
222) ju zhi suo he sa ni

223) di li e bi ti shi po li duo
224) zha zha ying jia
225) mo he ba she lu tuo la
226) di li pu po na
227) man cha la
228) wu xin
229) suo xi di
230) bo po du
231) mo mo
232) yin tu na mo mo xie
III.
233) la she po ye
234) zhu la ba ye
235) e qi ni po ye
236) wu tuo jia po ye
237) pi sha po ye
238) she sa duo la po ye
239) po la zhao jie la po ye
240) tu shai cha po ye
241) e she ni po ye
242) e jia la
243) mi li zhu po ye
244) tuo la ni bu mi jian
245) bo qie bo tuo po ye
246) wu la jia po duo po ye
247) la she tan cha po ye
248) nuo qie po ye
249) pi tiao dan po ye
250) su bo la na po ye
251) yao cha jie la he
252) la cha si jie la he
253) bi li duo jie la he

254) pi she zhe jie la he

255) bu duo jie la he

256) jiu pan cha jie la he

257) bu dan na jie la he

258) jia zha bu dan na jie la he

259) xi qian du jie la he

260) e bo xi mo la jie la he

261) wu tan mo tuo jie la he

262) che ye jie la he

263) xi li po di jie la he

264) she duo he li nan

265) jie po he li nan

266) lu di la he li nan

267) mang suo he li nan

268) mi tuo he li nan

269) mo she he li nan

270) she duo he li nyu

271) shi bi duo he li nan

272) pi duo he li nan

273) po duo he li nan

274) e shu zhe he li nyu

275) zhi duo he li nyu

276) di shan sa pi shan

277) sa po jie la he nan

278) pi tuo ye she

279) chen tuo ye mi

280) ji la ye mi

281) bo li ba la zhe jia

282) qi li dan

283) pi tuo ye she

284) chen tuo ye mi

285) ji la ye mi

286) cha yan ni
287) qi li dan
288) pi tuo ye she
289) chen tuo ye mi
290) ji la ye mi
291) mo he bo shu bo dan ye
292) lu tuo la
293) qi li dan
294) pi tuo ye she
295) chen tuo ye mi
296) ji la ye mi
297) nuo la ye na
298) qi li dan
299) pi tuo ye she
300) chen tuo ye mi
301) ji la ye mi
302) dan tuo qie lu cha xi
303) qi li dan
304) pi tuo ye she
305) chen tuo ye mi
306) ji la ye mi
307) mo he jia la
308) mo dan li qie na
309) qi li dan
310) pi tuo ye she
311) chen tuo ye mi
312) ji la ye mi
313) jia bo li jia
314) qi li dan
315) pi tuo ye she
316) chen tuo ye mi
317) ji la ye mi

318) she ye jie la
319) mo du jie la
320) sa po la tuo suo da na
321) qi li dan
322) pi tuo ye she
323) chen tuo ye mi
324) ji la ye mi
325) zhe du la
326) po qi ni
327) qi li dan
328) pi tuo ye she
329) chen tuo ye mi
330) ji la ye mi
331) pi li yang qi li zhi
332) nan tuo ji sha la
333) qie na bo di
334) suo xi ye
335) qi li dan
336) pi tuo ye she
337) chen tuo ye mi
338) ji la ye mi
339) na jie na she la po na
340) qi li dan
341) pi tuo ye she
342) chen tuo ye mi
343) ji la ye mi
344) e luo han
345) qi li dan
346) pi tuo ye she
347) chen tuo ye mi
348) ji la ye mi
349) pi duo la qie

350) qi li dan
351) pi tuo ye she
352) chen tuo ye mi
353) ji la ye mi
354) ba she la bo ni
355) ju xi ye ju xi ye
356) jia di bo di
357) qi li dan
358) pi tuo ye she
359) chen tuo ye mi
360) ji la ye mi
361) la cha wang
362) po qie fan
363) yin tu na mo mo xie

IV.

364) po qie fan
365) sa dan duo bo da la
366) na mo cui du di
367) e xi duo na la la jia
368) bo la po
369) xi pu zha
370) pi jia sa dan duo bo di li
371) shi fo la shi fo la
372) tuo la tuo la
373) pin tuo la pin tuo la
374) chen tuo chen tuo
375) hu xin hu xin
376) pan zha pan zha pan zha pan zha pan zha
377) suo he
378) xi xi pan
379) e mo jia ye pan
380) e bo la ti he duo pan

381) po la bo la tuo pan
382) e su la
383) pi tuo la
384) bo jia pan
385) sa po ti pi bi pan
386) sa po na qie bi pan
387) sa po yao cha bi pan
388) sa po qian ta po bi pan
389) sa po bu dan na bi pan
390) jia zha bu dan na bi pan
391) sa po tu lang zhi di bi pan
392) sa po tu si bi li
393) qi shai di bi pan
394) sa po shi po li bi pan
395) sa po e bo xi mo li bi pan
396) sa po she la po na bi pan
397) sa po di di ji bi pan
398) sa po dan mo tuo ji bi pan
399) sa po pi tuo ye
400) la shi zhe li bi pan
401) she ye jie la
402) mo du jie la
403) sa po la tuo suo tuo ji bi pan
404) pi di ye
405) zhe li bi pan
406) zhe du la
407) fu qi ni bi pan
408) ba she la
409) ju mo li
410) pi tuo ye
411) la shi bi pan
412) mo he bo la ding yang

413) yi qi li bi pan
414) ba she la shang jie la ye
415) bo la zhang qi la she ye pan
416) mo he jia la ye
417) mo he mo dan li jia na
418) na mo suo jie li duo ye pan
419) bi shai na bei ye pan
420) bo la he mo ni ye pan
421) e qi ni ye pan
422) mo he jie li ye pan
423) jie la tan chi ye pan
424) mie dan li ye pan
425) lao dan li ye pan
426) zhe wen cha ye pan
427) jie luo la dan li ye pan
428) jia bo li ye pan
429) e di mu zhi duo
430) jia shi mo she nuo
431) po si ni ye pan
432) yan ji zhi
433) sa tuo po xie
434) mo mo yin tu na mo mo xie

V.

435) tu shai zha zhi duo
436) e mo dan li zhi duo
437) wu she he la
438) qie po he la
439) lu di la he la
440) po suo he la
441) mo she he la
442) she duo he la
443) shi bi duo he la

444) ba liao ye he la

445) qian tuo he la

446) bu shi bo he la

447) po la he la

448) po xie he la

449) bo bo zhi duo

450) tu shai zha zhi duo

451) lao tuo la zhi duo

452) yao cha jie la he

453) la cha suo jie la he

454) bi li duo jie la he

455) pi she zhe jie la he

456) bu duo jie la he

457) jiu pan cha jie la he

458) xi qian tuo jie la he

459) wu dan mo tuo jie la he

460) che ye jie la he

461) e bo sa mo la jie la he

462) zhai que ge

463) cha qi ni jie la he

464) li fo di jie la he

465) she mi jia jie la he

466) she ju ni jie la he

467) mu tuo la

468) nan di jia jie la he

469) e lan po jie la he

470) qian du bo ni jie la he

471) shi fa la

472) yin jia xi jia

473) zhui di yao jia

474) dan li di yao jia

475) zhe tu tuo jia

476) ni ti shi fa la

477) bi shan mo shi fa la

478) bo di jia

479) bi di jia

480) shi li shai mi jia

481) suo ni bo di jia

482) sa po shi fa la

483) shi lu ji di

484) mo tuo pi da lu zhi jian

485) e qi lu qian

486) mu que lu qian

487) jie li tu lu qian

488) jie la he

489) jie lan jie na shu lan

490) dan duo shu lan

491) qi li ye shu lan

492) mo mo shu lan

493) ba li shi po shu lan

494) bi li shai zha shu lan

495) wu tuo la shu lan

496) jie zhi shu lan

497) ba xi di shu lan

498) wu lu shu lan

499) chang qie shu lan

500) he xi duo shu lan

501) ba tuo shu lan

502) suo fang ang qie

503) bo la zhang qie shu lan

504) bu duo bi duo cha

505) cha qi ni

506) shi po la

507) tuo tu lu jia

508) jian du lu ji zhi

509) po lu duo pi

510) sa bo lu

511) he ling qie

512) shu sha dan la

513) suo na jie la

514) pi sha yu jia

515) e qi ni

516) wu tuo jia

517) mo la pi la

518) jian duo la

519) e jia la

520) mi li du

521) da lian bu jia

522) di li la zha

523) bi li shai zhi jia

524) sa po na ju la

525) si yin qie bi

526) jie la li yao cha

527) dan la chu

528) mo la shi

529) fei di shan

530) suo pi shan

531) xi dan duo bo da la

532) mo he ba she lu

533) shai ni shan

534) mo he bo lai zhang qi lan

535) ye bo tu tuo

536) she yu she nuo

537) bian da li na

538) pi tuo ye

539) pan tan jia lu mi

540) di shu
541) pan tan jia lu mi
542) bo la pi tuo
543) pan tan jia lu mi
544) da zhi tuo
545) nan
546) e na li
547) pi she ti
548) pi la
549) ba she la
550) tuo li
551) pan tuo pan tuo ni
552) ba she la bang ni pan
553) hu xin du lu yong pan
554) suo po he

Opening Verse on the Commentary
of the Shurangama Mantra
by Venerable Master Hsuan Hua

The Ultimately Durable King among Samadhis--
With a straight mind practice and study it,
and the Way-place can be reached.
Purify the karmas of body, mouth, and mind;
Sweep clean the thoughts of greed, hatred, and stupidity.
From sincerity comes a response;
clear certification is obtained.
From concentration one accomplishes
spiritual powers which are great.
Endowed with virtue, you have encountered
its magical, wonderful phrases.
At all times, never forget to glorify its magnificence.

The Chinese characters which stand for Shurangama are *leng yen*; *leng* means "edge"; *yen* means "adorned." But, basically, the two characters, *leng yen*, are transliterations of the Sanskrit, Shurangama. Shurangama means "ultimately firm and solid in all respects.

"The Ultimately Durable King among Samadhis"
This eight line verse will explain the meaning of the commentary on the Shurangama Mantra.

"With a straight mind, practice and study it"
One should cultivate and study with a straight-forward mind to arrive at one's aim.

"To reach the Way Place"
A straight-forward mind is the field of the Way. If you are devious and use a crooked mind in cultivating the Buddhadharma, you won't be able to obtain any benefit from this mantra.

"Purify the karmas of body, mouth, and mind"
When you cultivate this Dharma, you can't speak falsely. You can't always be saying things that aren't true. You must avoid the body karma of breaking the precepts against killing, stealing, and sexual misconduct. With your mouth, you shouldn't speak irresponsibly, lie, gossip, or use harmful speech. Your thoughts should be devoid of greed, anger, and stupidity. So, "purify the karmas of body, mouth, and mind." With the three kinds of karma purified, one unites and upholds. That is Dharani.

"Sweep clean the thoughts of greed, hatred and stupidity"
You must totally clean up thoughts of greed, thoughts of anger, and thoughts of stupidity. When the mind is totally clean, these are all gone.

"From sincerity comes a response; clear certification is obtained"
If you have sincerity, then you will get a great response. You can immediately certify to the power of this mantra. It's inconceivable.

"From concentration, one accomplishes spiritual powers which are great"
If you are totally concentrated in your mind, and your thoughts don't wander—if you don't have any extraneous thoughts—then you will be able to realize great spiritual power.

In the Shurangama Mantra there are five major sections, and in these sections there are more than thirty different sub-sections of Dharmas.
The five major Dharmas are: 1) the Dharma of Subduing; 2) the Dharma of Hooking; 3) the Dharma of Eradicating Disasters; 4) the Dharma of Increasing Benefit; and 5) the Dharma of Accomplishment and Auspiciousness. There are a lot of different kinds of Dharmas in this mantra.

"Endowed with virtue, you have encountered its magical, wonderful phrases"
To study this kind of Dharma you must have virtuous conduct. If your conduct were not virtuous, you basically wouldn't even meet up with it. And, even if you were to meet up with it, you wouldn't understand it. This is an efficacious language; these are subtle, wonderful, profound phrases.

"At all times, never forget to glorify its magnificence"
You should never forget to cultivate this Dharma. Be sincere and concentrate and never forget to glorify the Buddhadharma, bringing it to great prosperity, so that the Buddhadharma will constantly remain in the world and be ever protected.

This is my very simple explanation of the general meaning of the Shurangama Mantra. Were I to speak about it in detail, I'd never finish. This is a dharma that is hard to encounter in hundreds of thousands of kalpas, so don't miss the opportunity! My explanations will be a very simple commentary on the Shurangama Mantra. If you want to understand it, you'll have to study it in detail yourself.

PART ONE

DHARMA TALKS

BY VENERABLE MASTER
HSUAN HUA

1

Explaining the Shurangama Mantra with My Blood, with My Sincerity

Whoever recites it will get a response. Vajra Treasury Bodhisattvas protect anyone who recites this mantra and uses it as a practice.

The Shurangama Mantra is the longest Buddhist mantra. We call it "magical words" because it is extremely efficacious and wonderful, so wonderful it is beyond words. Whoever recites it will get a response. Vajra Treasury Bodhisattvas protect anyone who recites this mantra and uses it as a practice. To do this mantra as a practice, we must, first of all, be sincere and become straightforward. We must cultivate and eliminate our desire for material objects, which means to be free of greed. Being able to eliminate desire and reaching real understanding, being sincere, and cultivating in the proper frame of mind, we would then experience tremendous miraculous results from doing this mantra as our practice.

Some people rashly claim that the Shurangama Mantra is as long as it is because it is composed of many short mantras. People who make such claims are worse than children, who in general, repeat what adults say thinking that will keep them from making mistakes.

The Shurangama Mantra starts by taking refuge with all the Buddhas of the Ten Directions who pervade all of space and the Dharma Realm, all Bodhisattvas of the Ten Directions who pervade all of space and the Dharma Realm, Arhats, sages of the First Fruit through the Fourth Fruit, and gods.

Taking refuge with gods does not mean that we are committed to emulating them; it just means that we respect them. Actually, monastics do not need to pay homage to anyone, in fact, gods are supposed to pay homage to members of the fully-ordained Sangha. So why should we pay respects to the gods? Gods pay homage to those with virtue and those who have cultivated. No one should be arrogant and say, "You know, all the Dharma-protecting gods bow to me!" Even if we were to have perfected our virtues, we should not be conceited and think we are better than anyone else. Even then, we should be as if we have none of whatever it is we have, emptied of what is actually there. We must not be attached to our virtues. We must never be satisfied with the amount of knowledge we have. This way, we are cultivators. Cultivators who recite this mantra and do this mantra as a practice should venerate the gods and good spirits—even the bad spirits. That is, we should curb our habit of arrogance.

The benefits from chanting the Shurangama Mantra as a practice are ineffable. I do not want to tell you what these benefits are exactly, because if I were to tell you and you recite it out of greed, then what benefit could you possibly earn? You would not be doing it because you really want to recite and practice this mantra. If you really want to recite and practice the Shurangama Mantra, then you should regard it as important as eating, putting on clothes, and sleeping. This is what we should do. If not, we can just forget about getting our prayers answered. Once we think about it, it is a false thought. How could we indulge such ideas when we have not perfected our skill? That would be like a child who is already thinking about running when he has barely learned to sit up. He cannot even walk, yet he wants to run. Now, why does he think in this way? It is because he does not understand. And then once he knows how to run around, he wants to fly. You think he could do it? Impossible! In the same way, why do you think about what is impossible? You are not a bird; you have not grown wings and yet you want to fly? This is a huge false thought.

The same principle applies to holding the Shurangama Mantra. Cultivation is just cultivation. Do not harbor thoughts of wanting something out of it. "I am definitely going to get something," we think. What are we going to get? "I am not going to die." No, when the time comes, you will die just the same. There is no way to escape death. That was a false thought you had. But, if you cultivate seriously and certify to sagehood, then you will really end birth and death, and that counts! But, if we were to think, "I do not want to die! I do not want to die! I do not want to die! I am going to guard this stinkin' skin bag of mine." We may guard it all we want but when the time comes, we have to say goodbye and go away.

The Shurangama Mantra is a magical language. Each phrase that you recite has its own special effect. But you should not dwell on its effect. Do not think, "Why have I been reciting it for so long without any tangible results?" When you eat, you appease your hunger for the time being; how could you expect to be full forever? When tomorrow comes, you still have to eat. Doing the Shurangama Mantra as a practice is just this way. Do it as a practice every day and you will not have wasted any effort. You will experience its effect eventually.

Whoever recites the Shurangama Mantra as a practice has to his left and right eighty-four thousand Vajra Treasury Bodhisattvas who are always guarding him. That is true. However, when you recite this mantra, it is best that you do not indulge in false thinking. If you keep on having random thoughts when you recite, the Vajra Treasury Bodhisattvas will think, "This person is really useless and has no future. He is wasting my time." You have to be careful because Dharma-protecting Bodhisattvas can get angry and they do.

The most important thing about doing the Shurangama

Mantra as a practice is that we observe the precepts purely. If we do not observe the precepts, no matter what we cultivate and however we recite, there will be no response. If we observe the precepts and are free of jealousy, obstructiveness, greed, anger and delusion, then we will enjoy a major response and reap a tremendous amount of benefit when we recite the mantra. I will say this, reciting the Shurangama Mantra and using it as a practice is more valuable than dealing in gold. The Shurangama Mantra, recited once, is as valuable as millions and millions of ounces of gold. But of course, you should not uphold the mantra out of greed.

I cannot say that my way of lecturing the Shurangama Mantra is poor. But I can say that nobody has ever lectured it in this way before. I composed a four-line verse for every line of the Great Compassion Mantra, which describe the function and power of the given line of mantra. Now, of course, in a four-line verse we can hardly explain all of the power in a given line of the mantra, because the wonderful meaning of the mantra is inexhaustible. Every single syllable and phrase of that mantra has boundless benefits. Obviously this is more than a four-line verse can contain. Although we cannot describe it in its entirety, we can talk about it a bit. But that bit of description will only be a small percentage of all the meaning contained there within. Four-line verses are easy to remember. From the simple, you can enter the profound. From the few, you can enter into the many. From what's near, you can go to what's far. In this way, you can deeply enter the meaning of the mantra.

Actually, one cannot talk about the mantra or try to explain it. But we will try to do it anyway, the purpose being a modest spur to induce someone to come forward with his valuable contribution. That is why I am explaining the Shurangama Mantra now. It should not concern you whether these four lines are meaningful enough, or even totally accurate; just realize that they come from my heart. You can say they are my sweat and blood. I explain the Shurangama Mantra with sincerity. And I hope after listening, you will truly understand the meaning of this mantra, even more deeply and more profoundly than I do. I hope the magnitude of your comprehension surpasses mine. That is why I say this is a modest spur to induce other valuable contributions. I hope you discover your wisdom and illumine the Sutra Treasury, so that your wisdom becomes like the sea. People who study Buddhism should always aim for the best. Always try to be better than you were before. You should not say, "I understand it, but I do not know how to cultivate it." It must actually be cultivated! If you do not cultivate, then no matter how much you know, it does not make sense at all. It is of no use. You must cultivate seriously. Put your feet firmly on the ground, and actually put the teaching into practice. Do not be so foolish as to steal a bell with your ears plugged—cheating yourself and cheating others. My wisdom and my mind are introduced in these four-line verses that I authored. I am explaining the Shurangama Mantra sincerely in the hope that all of you will understand more.

Recite the Shurangama Mantra to Help the Universe

If we recite the Shurangama Mantra, we can help heaven and earth, and aid in curing the universe of its violence and ills.

People get sick, the earth gets sick, and so do the heavens. We on the earth may not know it, but there are often sicknesses in the heavens. If we recite the Shurangama Mantra, we can help heaven and earth, and aid in curing the universe of its violence and ills. The recitation has an imperceptibly good effect on heaven and earth and everything in general.

We do not recite only one line of the Shurangama Mantra. It is in sections. Although each line has its individual meaning, the lines are related. The Shurangama Mantra contains little sections. Learn the start and finish of these little segments.

It does not matter what Dharma door you practice, you have to pay attention to your virtue first. If you do not have enough virtue, you will face demonic obstacles. You have to develop merit and virtue. Merit means you protect the Bodhimanda—you work tirelessly and uncomplainingly. Virtue means you do not obstruct other people—you do not bring distress to others. No matter what practice you cultivate, you will gain nothing from it unless you change your temper and stop your worries. We need to develop merit and virtue once we entered monastic life. With that, it will be easier to cultivate any practice. It is said:

> Go too fast and you will trip.
> Dally, and you will fall behind.
> Never rush and never dally
> And you will get there right on time.

In cultivating, it is easy to be vigorous in the beginning, it is hard to keep it up as you go along. Make sure you are committed for the long-term and refuse to retreat.

There are various reasons for dangerous states that occur during meditation, not merely one reason. Some people wish to cultivate but they are too selfish, their view of self is too deeply rooted and they never forget themselves. They are always selfish and self-seeking. Selfishness makes it easy to become possessed by a demon. Real cultivation of the Bodhisattva Way is done without anxiety. One does not seek for quick ways to get enlightened and become an "instant" Buddha. Someone likely to become possessed may be curious, wishes to be different, hopes for spiritual powers to experience some states different than others.

If you were concentrating on your meditation and entertaining no other thoughts, then demons would be unable to enter even if you wanted them to possess you. Your ability to significantly diminish your false thoughts and deviant views keeps them at bay. People become possessed because of deviant ideas and views. If you are just, fair, and selfless, if you are not in a big hurry and not trying to surpass others, if you just concentrate and work hard on your mind, then no demons will get you. Meditation is not dangerous. I mean, eating is not dangerous, but if you eat too much your stomach may burst or if you eat too little you will not be nourished. You can get sick easily if you are greedy for fine tastes. You do not get sick from eating but from not eating properly. The same applies to meditation.

Magical Words
that Avert Doomsday

If just one person knows how to recite the Shurangama Mantra, this world will not become extinct nor will the Dharma.

I am now explaining the Shurangama Mantra. In a hundred, thousand, myriad eons, no one has explained the Shurangama Mantra even once. It is not easy to lecture it even once. I am lecturing it for you now, but it is not for sure anyone understands it. Some may feel that they understand it, but they do not really understand it. Some may feel they already understand it, so they do not pay attention, but that is just the same as not understanding it. The Shurangama Mantra is a force that sustains heaven and earth. It delays their extinction. It is the very spiritual force which prevents the world from coming to an end. I have said that as long as one person can recite the Shurangama Mantra, the world

11

will not be destroyed and the Dharma will not come to an end. When not a single person can recite the Shurangama Mantra, the Buddhadharma will become extinct.

Demons in the heavens and proponents of externalist ways are now spreading rumors that the Shurangama Sutra and Mantra are false. To destroy people's faith in the Shurangama Mantra, heavenly demons send their demon sons and grandsons to spread rumors. If no one believes in the Mantra, no one will recite it. When no one recites it, the world will quickly come to an end. If we do not want the world to come to an end, we must read and recite the Shurangama Mantra and Shurangama Sutra. By reciting the Shurangama Mantra every day, we are protected from harm. Even dangerous atom bombs and hydrogen bombs cannot touch us. So concentrate on reciting the Shurangama Mantra.

I am lecturing the Shurangama Mantra for you and no one necessarily understands it right now. But ten, a hundred, or a thousand years from now someone may come across this very shallow commentary on the Shurangama Mantra and develop a deep understanding of it. Those of you who hear these Shurangama Mantra lectures should not think it is so easy. Although these four-line verses seem very simple, they flow forth from my heart. They are definitely not plagiarized from any other book or commentary. Since you are studying with me, I am offering verses, whether good or not, written from my views on and understanding of the Shurangama Mantra. If you really want to understand the Shurangama Mantra, then you should pay close attention while you study it. Do not let this time go by in vain.

Door to liberation, dispeller of disasters, bestower of great joy,

The Foremost Shurangama Dharma is incomparable in the world.

All obstacles ultimately end when enlightenment prevails.

Rejecting the common, one ascends to sagehood, and meshes with true understanding.

Insincerity Means Ineffectiveness

What is sincerity? No doubts. The power from really believing in the mantra is inconceivable. That powerful faith in the mantra will bring success.

In cultivating all Dharma doors, be it reciting sutras or upholding mantras, one must be sincere. Fast, maintain morality, and cleanse the body. Be clear and pure in body and mind. Eradicate all false thinking as you cultivate a Dharma door. That way you will mesh with the Tao, like an echo of a sound. If you are not sincere, no matter how efficacious the Mantra is, it will not work for you. So we say: When the mind is sincere, the mantra is effective. If you are not sincere, it will not be magical.

What is sincerity? It means having no doubts and having true faith in the inconceivable power of the Mantra—faith that its power will never fail. If you can truly be sincere, then your cultivation will succeed. Sometimes people may cultivate for a long time and get no response. Then they may start to think, "Is the Buddhadharma ineffective? What is going on? I am not getting any results." It is not that the Mantra is not efficacious. You are not succeeding because you are not sincere. You are merely bundling your way through it, going through the motions. You have not brought forth true sincerity. So it is most important that those who recite the Shurangama Mantra be sincere.

There are many ghosts, spirits, dragons and gods of the Eightfold Division in the Shurangama Mantra. As soon as you recite a ghost king's name, all his retinue must listen to the teachings; they would not dare to disobey the rules. Therefore monastics recite the Shurangama Mantra every day to help free the world from untimely disasters and calamities, bringing peace to the world. By holding morning and evening ceremonies, monastics imperceptibly enable all beings to be safe, peaceful and happy.

When we recite the Shurangama Mantra, the polluted air

in the world is cleansed. Our recitation of the Shurangama Mantra eradicates the contagious diseases in the area. If there is poison in the area, it will be eliminated as soon as the Shurangama Mantra is recited. That is how great the benefit is! Therefore you should not take the Shurangama Mantra lightly. It is best to recite the whole mantra. If you cannot, then just reciting a certain part of it is still very powerful. Do not mistake gold for copper. All of you who study Buddhism must memorize and uphold the Shurangama Mantra.

Endlessly miraculous and mysterious,
these syllables are hard to decipher.

And yet, this vajra secret language wells
forth from our own nature.

The Shurangama Mantra, thus wrought
with stunning efficacy,

Opens access to the Five Eyes and
Six Penetrations for sages and people.

Set a Goal to Recite the Shurangama Mantra for the World

Someone who studies the Shurangama Mantra is a transformation of the Buddha, not simply a transformation of the Buddha, but the transformation of a Buddha from the top of the Buddha, a transformational Buddha among transformational Buddhas.

Every line of the Shurangama Mantra contains boundless meanings and functions. People who recite and uphold it should bring forth a vast resolve. You should resolve to recite and uphold it for the sake of the whole world and transfer merit and virtue to all beings. Your enormous resolve will reap enormous reward because you are not selfish and working for yourself. A passage from the "Essay on Great Reform and Repentance" illustrates this point: "I now resolve not to seek for myself the rewards of humans and gods, of Sound Hearers and Those Enlightened by Conditions, up to and including those of the positions of Bodhisattvas in the provisional vehicle. I only rely on the most supreme vehicle as I bring forth the Bodhi resolve. I vow to join all beings as we simultaneously attain Anuttarasamyaksambodhi," leaving suffering and attaining bliss.

We must become proficient in our studies of Buddhism. Avoid learning about Buddhism on the one hand and creating offense karma on the other, mixing good and bad together. If you study the Buddhadharma not for the sake of benefiting others, but for the sake of benefiting yourself, then you are mixing the good with the bad. When you first started studying Buddhism, you might have intended to benefit others, but as time passes, your old habit of selfishness crops up.

If you study the Buddhadharma and gamble at the same time, you are mixing good and bad. If you study the Buddhadharma and still try to cheat or harm others and benefit yourself, you are also mixing good and bad. If you rely on your connections in Buddhist circles to deal in disreputable business, to the point of cheating and stealing, you are getting good and bad karma all jumbled up. You have to stop such activities, otherwise you will be stuck in that mixture of good and evil karma and you will never be able to transcend the Triple Realm.

Cultivators should avoid, on the one hand, cultivating in the monastery, and on the other, having false thoughts. That kind of behavior is neither completely good nor completely evil. Within the good there is bad and within the bad there is some good. But in the future when you undergo retribution, it will be extremely complicated.

We may wonder why monastics suffer abuse by their government. Although this life they are able to be monastics, they must pay for evil deeds they did in their previous periods of cultivation. If in the past, they confiscated other's wealth or usurped property, or took people's lives, then in their present lives, they have to undergo like retribution. There is no guarantee of their safety or belongings. Even though they are monastics, they may not escape alive, let alone with their property.

Basically, after one enters monastic life, one should not have any property to speak of. The reason that some monastics wander about in a desperate plight is because they planted improper causes in the past. To pay back for what they have done, they are born in war-infested countries and have to undergo tremendous suffering and abuse. I bring their situation up to give us a living example of the workings of the Dharma. We should return the light and look inside. Now, while cultivating, be careful not to make those kinds of mistakes, and in the future you can avoid such disasters. To avoid them, make sure that you are clear about the causes that you are planting. Do not be caught in a flurry of confusion when you face the retributions. It is said, "If what is done while planting causes is not true, the results will be twisted, too." For residents and visitors of the City of Ten Thousand Buddhas, be very careful. Be cautious while you cultivate so as to avoid regrets in the future.

Sincerely Practice
the Shurangama Mantra

If you are focused intently upon cultivation of the Shurangama Mantra, you will certainly realize the Shurangama Samadhi.

Be true and sincere as you cultivate the Shurangama Dharma. What is sincerity? You must cultivate the Shurangama Mantra to the point that you forget time and space. Is it day or night? You do not know. Have you eaten or not? You are unaware. Have you slept or not? You forget. Everything is gone. One thought is as long as limitless eons; limitless eons are encompassed in one thought. If you have that kind of energy and spirit, to the point of forgetting whether you have eaten or slept because you are focused intently upon cultivation of the Shurangama Mantra, you will certainly realize the Shurangama Samadhi. If you cannot be that way, then you are not genuinely cultivating the Shurangama

Dharma-door.

Not only should you cultivate the Shurangama Mantra like that, you should cultivate any Dharma-door that way— to the point that while standing you do not realize you are standing; while sitting you do not realize you are sitting; when thirsty you do not realize you are thirsty; when hungry you do not realize you are hungry. And you comment, "That sounds like that being totally out-of-it!" You need to be just that stupid, and then,

> When you can become like an old fool,
>   you have actually become really clever.
> When you cultivate to the point of stupidity,
>   your ability is seen.

If you can become stupid like that, then no matter what Dharma-door you cultivate, you will attain Samadhi or some level of achievement.

It is just because you cannot be stupid that you cannot genuinely and deeply enter the state of samadhi. So you have been cultivating all this time, but you do not mesh with your practice. You should cultivate to the point that you do not even know if you are alive or dead. You should reach the point in your practice where you do not even know if you are breathing or not. Some people think such depth of practice is too scary. If you are afraid, then hurry up and turn away, stop learning. In this world, you never get something for nothing. Nothing is that easy to get. So it is said,

> If it did not endure bitter cold that chills the bone,
> The plum blossom would not be so fragrant.

We who cultivate the spiritual path should be like that, too.

Outside observers often say that the City of Ten Thousand Buddhas is a place where the practice is bitterly difficult. I absolutely disagree with that kind of rumor. Here at the City of Ten Thousand Buddhas we do not engage in bitter cultivation; we practice blissful cultivation. Whoever cultivates, whoever undergoes bitterness, does so because he or she wants to. We are not forced into it. We are more than willing to put down the false in order to get back to the truth. So it is said:

> If you cannot forsake the false,
>   you cannot achieve the true.
> If you cannot give up death,
>   you cannot exchange it for birth.

Cultivation is not like some worldly methods where you can use some trick to get what you are after. No. It does not work that way. You cannot do that when you cultivate. You cannot pull any tricks. The only way to achieve success is to honestly and genuinely cultivate. If you have a hair's worth of phoniness, then you will not succeed. So at every turn you have to work hard at being real. Bear what others cannot bear; Yield where others cannot yield. If you can be perpetually vigorous, during 24 hours of the day, you will receive some good news. The Buddhas of the ten directions will send you a telegram, saying "Good, indeed! Good, indeed! You are a part of Buddhism!" But this telegram from the Buddhas of the ten directions is not like the telegrams people send each other, which are composed of words. This is a message of one mind leaving an imprint on another's mind. When it happens, the lights of both reflect each other and the minds of both tally with each other. At that point, you will uncover great wisdom, obtain great eloquence, and attain great peace. Then, "the work of the great person is accomplished." You will have done what had to be done.

Someone who Studies
the Shurangama Mantra
is a Transformation of the Buddha

If you master the Shurangama Mantra, the gods will not dare to counter you. If you mastered the Shuragama Mantra, you would dare to counter the gods.

There is a saying that goes "One who can recite the Great Compassion Mantra dares to fight with King Yama. Ghosts and spirits do not dare to fight someone who can recite the Great Compassion Mantra." If you can recite the Great Compassion Mantra, you can fight King Yama, and he will not be able to defend himself. And why would the ghosts and spirits leave you alone? It would not be because you have a nasty temper, but because you have real power and real authority. A person with virtue and morality will be treated with courtesy by King Yama and the ghosts and spirits. They would not fear you and stay away because you have a nasty temper. The Great Compassion Mantra has this power, and the Shurangama Mantra also has this power. It has even more power! We say, "If you master the Shurangama Mantra, the gods will not dare to counter you. If you master the Shurangama Mantra, you will dare to counter the gods." "Is the Shurangama Mantra unreasonable or specious distortion?" you ask. No. In fact, if you can recite the Shurangama Mantra, you will be wealthy in your next seven lives, possibly among the top wealthy people or becoming American oil magnates. "If I had known this, I would have started learning it long ago, so I could do compete with God and be rich for seven lives!"

If your motives are so petty, you would be better off not studying the mantra. Seven lifetimes pass in a blink of an eye, and even if you win in your battle with God, you are still on the turning wheel of rebirth. Ultimately, you should aim for Buddhahood, the supreme, proper enlightenment of Bodhi. Neither your mind nor your intent should be so petty. Actually, the Shurangama Mantra is equivalent to the Buddha's transformation body. Not only is it a transformation of the Buddha, it is the transformation Buddha above the crown of the Buddha, the transformation Buddha within transformation Buddhas. If one can genuinely hold the Shurangama Mantra, then for forty yojanas around there will be no calamities, and all inauspiciousness will be changed to auspiciousness.

You acquire it only because of Great Virtue & Great Goodness

The Shurangama Mantra is the wonderful Dharma that is difficult to encounter in billions of eons. You should pay strict attention to each and every line. Do not treat it as if it were something ordinary.

Pay particular attention to every line of the Shurangama Mantra. Do not treat it as if it were something ordinary. This wonderful Dharma is difficult to encounter in billions of eons. Perhaps you think many people lecture on the Shurangama Mantra, but in fact no one lectures it.

> The pervasive illumination of three lights
>   permeates three forces.
> You may never come upon this mantra in Jambudvipa
>   or the world beyond.
> Possessing great virtue and great goodness

will allow us to encounter it.
Deficient virtue and goodness will keep us
from ever understanding it.

—verse by Master Hua

As I explain the Shurangama Mantra now, you should pay strict attention to each and every line. Do not treat it as if it were something ordinary.

This wonderful Dharma is difficult to encounter in billions of eons. Perhaps you believe lots of people lecture on the Shurangama Mantra; actually no one is lecturing it. People dare not even believe in the Shurangama Mantra when they hear it! Some people are afraid that they do not understand what the Shurangama Mantra really means. Well, ask me and see if I understand. I do not understand completely either. I only understand a little bit and I have put this little bit into verses as an attempt to explain the mantra. Do not miss this opportunity to study the mantra if you wish to learn Buddhadharma.

I have more than 20 disciples in Hong Kong who constantly asked me to explain the Shurangama Mantra but I never agreed to it. When I got to the United States though, I started lecturing on the Shurangama Sutra during the first summer retreat. I lectured that Sutra for 96 days, resting only on Saturdays. Later I also lectured on the Sixth Patriarch Platform Sutra, Vajra Sutra, Dharma Flower

Sutra, Earth Store Sutra and then Flower Adornment Sutra. All these took nine and a half years—though I had planned ten years for these. Since this is rocket age, I finished half a year earlier. I did not want to lecture on anything else after I finished the Flower Adornment Sutra.

But then you asked me to lecture on the Shurangama Mantra and I thought I might as well tell you what I know. Thus we begin these lectures on the Shurangama Mantra, which is itself inconceivable. Do not let any word or any line slip by. I do not know how people in the audience feel, but I never take days off when it comes to lecturing. You do not need to ask, "Venerable Master, will you be lecturing today?" Yes, except for when I am not here. If I am here I will definitely lecture. If I do not lecture, I will not eat. Even after lecturing, I only eat 80% full. If I become too fat, people will criticize, "Those monks only eat all day. They get big and fat because they do not do anything." Is it not better to eat less? I believe I am not the only one who eats little. The residents at the City of Ten Thousand Buddhas all eat very little. They may look emaciated but they are hard to the core. I, a hard-core teacher, have created a bunch of little hard cores. It is alright that we do not eat; it is okay to not dress well; it is not a problem to go without

sleep. We do not consider any of these things an issue!

Cultivation is like climbing a hundred foot pole: it is easy to slide down but hard to climb up, as hard as trying to step onto sky. We can easily become attached to demonic obstructions whenever we cannot get beyond a state. It can happen in the space of a thought. One wrong thought, one thought of evil, lets the demons into your heart. With proper thoughts, the Buddhas become one with you. That is why the Sixth Patriarch Sutra says, "The Buddha is in the room when our thoughts are proper; demons are in the hall when our thoughts are deviant." This is the underlying principle.

As long as we have a bit of contention, greed, wishful thinking, thoughts of selfishness or self-benefit, the demons are sitting in the hall. If we are free of contention, greed, wishful thinking, selfishness and self-interest, then no demons or ghosts have a way to slip in and disturb us. If we do not fight with anyone, demons cannot get to us. If we are not greedy for bargains, supernatural powers or other advantages, then we cannot be enticed by any false seductions.

Furthermore, wishing for nothing inside and out, we forget everything, including this self and others. Forgetting ourselves and others, dharmas perish. In addition, be altruistic; be selfless with regard to everything. Stop wanting more benefit for yourself and denying others benefit. Being this way, demon kings cannot touch us. When we are not constantly thinking about what benefits us, the spells of demons and ghosts do not work. This is the best mantra to use against demons and cults. Do these five things well and there are no demons. How come they can wedge themselves into a crack? It is because you still have wishful thinking, you still have greed, contention, selfishness, or self-interest. They take advantage of such opportunities and dig their way into your heart, making your head unclear and your wisdom die out.

The Proper Dharma Exists in the Presence of the Shurangama Mantra

The Shurangama Mantra is the King of Mantras. It is also the longest Mantra among mantras. This mantra has a profound effect on the flourishing or decaying of the Buddhadharma as a whole.

The Shurangama Mantra is called the "Unsurpassed Mahasitatapatra Spiritual Mantra". Maha is Sanskrit and means big. Its substance, form and functions are all quite immense. Its substance covers the ten directions. Its immense functions reach all of space and the Dharma Realm. As for form, it has none. What form is there to a mantra? It has no form and it is not devoid of form. It could also be said to be useless and yet it is not devoid of any usage. It functions anywhere in space and the Dharma Realm, which makes its functions immense. The mantra's form is immense and its substance is immense too. This is what is meant by "maha".

Sitata is also Sanskrit, which means the color white. It also means purity, being free of defilement. Therefore it is said, "Form apart from all defilements is said to be white." The Shurangama Mantra is a white and pure Dharma. Patra is also Sanskrit and means canopy. This is a metaphor of how a canopy can shade all things and all virtuous individuals. Anyone with virtue will encounter this Dharma. Those without virtue will not encounter it. "The pervasive illumination of three lights permeates three forces." Most people think the "three lights" are the sun, moon and stars. But the sun, the moon and the stars are the three kinds of lights outside. By reciting the Shurangama Mantra, we can make our internal lights shine. There are lights in our body, lights in our mouth and lights in our mind. The three karmas of body, mouth and mind all emit light. Have you heard this before? I believe this is something you have never heard or seen.

The light our body emits is yellow. When we have cultivated successfully, the light becomes golden, beaming numerous rays of golden lights. When we first start to practice the Shurangama Mantra, the light is a pale yellow. After some time, it turns into a golden light. That is why it is said that when the Shurangama Mantra is cultivated successfully, infinite rays of pure golden lights touched with a purple tinge fill up the Dharma Realm.

The light that we release from our mouth is red in color.

The light that we emit from our mind is white. Though sometimes our mouth emits a yellow light too; sometimes green, sometimes black, and sometimes white. But this is only when one has cultivated this successfully.

Patra means nurturing myriad virtues. The great white canopy protects all those virtuous beings who uphold the Shurangama Mantra as a practice, hence, "The pervasive illumination of three lights permeates three forces." The three forces are heaven, earth and people. "You may never come upon these in Jambudvipa or the world beyond." We cannot find these lights anywhere in Jambudvipa except by doing the Shurangama Mantra as a practice. "Possessing great virtue and great goodness will allow us to encounter it." Only those with tremendous virtue and goodness learn about this practice. "Deficient virtue and goodness will keep us from ever understanding it." If we had no virtue and no merit from good deeds, we would miss it even if it were right in front of us. We may think gold is merely metal and diamond is merely glass, hence think the Shurangama Mantra quite average, no big deal. We do not know that it is a gem! We do not know that it is amazing! We do not know that the merit derived and the virtues deriving from the Shurangama Mantra are incredible.

Lights from the mind are lights from thoughts, which come from the Sixth Consciousness. Of course if we do not cultivate it, those lights will not function. If we cultivate, lights are emitted. Furthermore, lights described earlier not only come from the purified three karmas of body, mouth and mind, but red lights swirl about and linger too. Reciting the Shurangama Mantra, we naturally will have red lights surrounding us. That is why it says, "A thousand red lotuses protect the practitioner." These red lotuses emit red lights. "Who sits firmly mounted on a black unicorn." People who belong to this age of science are laughing their heads off when they hear this. But that is just as well. If they stop laughing, they will continue talking about science all the time. "Seeing this, the hordes of demons flee and hide." Any demons and ghosts who see the mighty and virtuous aspects of the Dharma body that is guarded by a thousand red lotuses will hide in a far-off place. "Dharma Master Ji, the Venerable, expressed this wonder." Beautiful purple lights and white lights coil about when we recite the Shurangama Mantra. Why do demons and ghosts not dare to come out when we recite the Shurangama Mantra? It has such tremendous power, so much so that no place throughout space and the Dharma Realm is exempt from being permeated with auspicious lights and energy. Anyone who recites the Shurangama Mantra is bolstering the amount of healthy energy in the universe. Commensurate strength comes from one person reciting the Shurangama Mantra or one hundred people, but either one puts the demons and ghosts in their place.

The Shurangama Mantra is the King of Mantras. It is also

the longest mantra around. This mantra has a profound effect on the flourishing or decaying of the Buddhadharma as a whole. If it ever comes to a point where no one in the world can recite the Shurangama Mantra, then the world will quickly fall to pieces, because the Proper Dharma no longer remains. Within the Proper Dharma, the Shurangama Sutra and the Shurangama Mantra are very important. The Shurangama Sutra was explained because of the Shurangama Mantra; it explains and praises the Shurangama Mantra. One of the passages in the Shurangama Sutra explains in great detail the how's of building a platform. If anyone wants to know more about this in detail, consult this passage of the Sutra text.

The Shurangama Mantra is called "The Light above the Crown of the Buddha." And, the crown of the Buddha is referring to the transformation Buddha on top of the crown that spoke the mantra. The Shurangama Mantra is subtle and inconceivably wonderful. Every phrase has a function. Every syllable contains mysterious wonder. It is inconceivable and ineffable. Light at the Buddha's crown also represents the strength of the Mantra, which shatters any kind of darkness and perfects people's merit and virtue. Accepting and maintaining the Shurangama Mantra as a practice, we will certainly become Buddhas in the future; we will certainly obtain the Unsurpassed, Proper, and Equal Right Enlightenment. We may recite it from memory, or, if we cannot remember it, we may read it from the book. If we recite this by heart all the time, we will melt our karmic obstacles from former lives. Our offenses from the past being wiped away is one of the wonderful functions of the Shurangama Mantra.

The next word in the title is "Unsurpassed." It is so high that nothing can reach it. It is superior, supreme, venerable, and lofty—beyond compare. There is nothing more honored; there is nothing higher. And that is what is meant by "unsurpassed." "Spiritual" means inconceivable and ineffable. It is an awesome efficaciousness that cannot be fathomed. A "mantra" brings about an intertwining of responses with the Way. When we recite the mantra, power comes forth. Recite the mantra and a response happens.

Reciting silently or aloud will diminish our words and thoughts.

Spreading the benefits and joys of the teaching will change the universe.

All methods that we use should be carried to ultimate completion.

No increase and no decrease indicate that we have reached Nirvana.

Earnestly Recite to Acquire
Wonderful Samadhi

All Buddhas of the ten directions are born from the Shurangama Mantra, which is why the Shurangama Mantra could be called the mother of Buddhas. There are so many advantages to the Shurangama Mantra, were I to try and describe all of them, I would not finish even in a few years. All Buddhas are born from the Shurangama Mantra; hence the Shurangama Mantra could be called the mother of Buddhas. It is because of the Shurangama Mantra that the Thus Come Ones throughout the ten directions realized the Unsurpassed, Proper, Pervasively Knowing and Proper Enlightenment. The Thus Come Ones of the ten directions can appear transformationally in as many countries as motes of dust. There they turn the Dharma wheel and teach living beings. They rub the heads of living beings and bestow predictions of future Buddhahood upon them. They uproot the various sufferings of beings and liberate them from all potential major and minor accidents at once. All this happens because of the power of the Shurangama Mantra.

If you wish to achieve arhatship, you must recite this mantra to avoid demonic situations. At a time when the Dharma is on the decline, anyone who can memorize and recite the Shurangama Mantra or tells others to read or recite the Shurangama Mantra will be immune from burning, drowning and poisoning. Any poison that enters the mouth of someone who recites the Shurangama Mantra will taste like sweet dew.

Someone who has accepted and upholds the Shurangama Mantra will not be born in a bad place; he cannot go even if he wants to. Why? The Shurangama Mantra will pull him back, telling him, "Do not go! Do not go!" Even if someone does not develop any blessings and virtue but does recite the Shurangama Mantra, all Thus Come Ones throughout the ten directions will give their merit and virtue to this individual. Is that a bargain? Recite the Shurangama Mantra and we will always become born when a Buddha is in the world, thereby cultivating with that Buddha.

If our thoughts are scattered and we cannot concentrate, we need only think about or silently recite the Shurangama Mantra that the Buddha spoke. That will cause the Vajra Treasury King Bodhisattvas to focus on us, following and quietly helping those of us who try to uphold the Shurangama Mantra despite our scattered minds. Those Bodhisattvas will help us reduce our chaotic thoughts bit by bit. Bit by bit we will acquire Samadhi power. They help us from behind the scenes so that we uncover our wisdom and concentrate our thoughts. We will then understand everything tracing back through eons equal to the number of sand grains in 84,000 Ganges Rivers.

When we become familiar enough with the Shurangama Mantra that we know it by heart and so that when we recite it, it seems to flow forth from our heart, then the Shurangama Mantra becomes our heart and our heart is just the Shurangama Mantra. Once our recitation is as smooth and constant as flowing water, we have reached the samadhi of upholding a mantra. At the minimum, for seven lives we will be as affluent as oil magnates, among the wealthiest people in the world. Someone says, "That is so great! I had better hurry up and study the Shurangama Mantra so that I can be rich for seven lives." Someone whose frame of mind is that narrow need not bother studying the Shurangama Mantra. Seven lives as a rich person pass in a blink of an eye too.

So what should we expect from knowing how to recite the Shurangama Mantra? We should expect to become a Buddha ultimately, realizing the Unsurpassed, Proper and Equal Enlightenment. Take care not to be petty. Actually someone who studies the Shurangama Mantra becomes a transformation of the Buddha. Not only is such a person a transformation of the Buddha, but a transformation Buddha from the crown of the Buddha—a transformation Buddha among transformation Buddhas. This is why the wonderful aspects about the Shurangama Mantra are inconceivable.

A large white canopy will hover above the crowns of those who really do the Shurangama Mantra as a practice. For the more skilled, that canopy will last as long as a thought and free an area of several thousand li (about one third of a mile) from any disasters. For the less skilled, that canopy will be there to protect you. If we were virtuous or preeminent monks, then an entire country would benefit from this one thought. There would be no disasters. If there were supposed to be disasters, then major ones would turn into minor ones and minor disasters would disappear.

Regardless of the type of disasters, be it famine, plague, contagious diseases, war or robbery—they vanish if we do the following: write out the Shurangama Mantra and place one at every entry through each side of the city, or its battery or blockhouse, and make everyone in the country pay homage to, welcome, and make obeisance to the Shurangama Mantra the way they would to a Buddha. Or require everyone to wear or keep a set of the Shurangama Mantra in their homes.

Wherever the Shurangama Mantra abides, the gods and dragons are happy. Such places do not experience storms or strong winds, their harvests are abundant, and everyone is safe and secure. So the merit and virtue of the Shurangama Mantra is inconceivable. It is wonderfully precise because we cannot imagine or conceive of such wonder.

A Symbol of the Proper Dharma —
the Shurangama Mantra

Being able to recite the Shurangama Mantra, we are helping sentient beings. Not being able to recite, we can't help sentient beings.

Each syllable and phrase of the Mantra has infinite meanings, and each meaning has infinite functions. Know that the Shurangama Mantra is the universe's magic text, the magical syllables among magical syllables, the mysterious among the mysterious, the best Dharma treasure. It is the treasure that saves all beings. It contains everything, from all Buddhas of the ten directions above to all beings in the Avici Hells below. The four types of sages and six types of ordinary beings all use the methods of the Shurangama Mantra. No Dharma realm goes beyond its bounds. All kinds of ghosts, spirits, Dharma protecting devas, Sound Hearers, Conditionally Enlightened Ones, and Buddhas are in the Shurangama Mantra.

The Shurangama Mantra names all the ghosts and spirit kings. Calling these ghosts and spirit kings by their names, their followings become subservient to us and comply. They do not dare to be wanton. Reciting the Shurangama Mantra every day can make the demons and ghosts well-behaved and they dare not come out to do harm. The substance of the Shurangama Mantra is complete and its functions are tremendous; they include all the lessons in Buddhism. If we understand the Shurangama Mantra, we understand the secrets and essence of Buddhism.

The mysteries of the universe, the incredible occurrences in the universe are in the Shurangama Mantra too. Were we to understand the Shurangama Mantra, we would have no need to study the secret school—be it the white school, black school, yellow school, or red school. We do not need to study any school. This is practice of samadhi at its most fundamental level. This is a secret Dharma in its ultimate state. Unfortunately, no one understands this kind of secret Dharma. Most people do not apply what they learn. They only know to read it but they do not know what it really means. That is acceptable, because we actually do not need to know what a mantra means; all we need to know is that it is an inconceivably magical text.

Being able to recite the Shurangama Mantra, we are helping

sentient beings. Not being able to recite, we cannot help sentient beings. Hurry up and learn the Shurangama Mantra well. Memorize it, study it well. Buddhists ought to do this. Those who wish to study and recite the Shurangama Mantra should set big goals to recite for the entire world so that all of their merit and virtue are dedicated to the world. In Buddhism, there is nothing more important than the Shurangama Mantra, for it is the symbol of the Proper Dharma. Wherever the Shurangama Mantra is, the proper Dharma is there; wherever there is no Shurangama Mantra, there is no proper Dharma. Those who cannot memorize the Shurangama Mantra are not qualified to be Buddhists.

The Shurangama Mantra is called "six month's stupor". It takes half a year to memorize it if a person recites it every day. Those of who can recite the Shurangama Mantra are people who have developed excellent roots of goodness over infinite eons. This is why we are able to read the Shurangama Mantra well, memorize it and never forget it. This is a sign of our roots of goodness. Without good roots, not only can we not read it, but we cannot even come into contact with the Shurangama Mantra. Someone who can come into contact with it, read, and memorize it is someone who has excellent roots of goodness.

The Shurangama Dharma is a practice difficult to encounter in billions of eons. Having studied and understood the power of one line, we must apply it. But we do not use it just because we heard how this Dharma has such tremendous magical responses, wonderful uses, and power. Someone who uses this Dharma without holding the precepts falls below the norm. Lacking any moral awareness, he casually kills, steals, engages in sexual misconduct, lies, takes intoxicants and yet dares to chant the five great mantras of the heart at critical moments. His behavior is defiled and he lacks virtue and yet he tries to order ghosts, spirits and Dharma protectors around. He will only create more offenses that way. He puts himself in harm's way—he will have an accident.

People who cultivate the Dharma must first adhere to the precepts and pay attention to virtue. They must not fight, not be greedy, not seek, not be selfish, not pursue self-benefit and not lie. Without enough moral virtue, one may pretend to be a king who issues imperial mandates, but these commands are useless. Most people nowadays only care about getting their own advantage, then even if they recite incessantly, their recitations will be ineffective.

While learning the Shurangama Dharma, we must be

proper. We need to keep our minds proper and devoid of any impure thoughts. We should not do anything impure. We must cultivate the practice of purity in thought after thought. If we cultivate the practice of the Shurangama Mantra on the one hand but do not observe the rules on the other, huge problems will occur. This is one point that everyone must understand.

If our thoughts are improper, our conduct will be improper. As a consequence of that, the Vajra Treasury Bodhisattvas will not respect you or protect you. The Buddhas and Bodhisattvas are compassionate and will not hurt sentient beings out of anger. But their attendants, such as all the Dharma protectors, gods and dragons, ghosts and spirits have huge tempers. Evil ghosts and spirits who observe someone who cultivates the mantra making transgressions will hurt him, make him ill at ease and give him a lot of problems. That individual will face all sorts of disasters and all kinds of retributions. This is no joke at all. Fast and bathe, and keep the mind clean by not entertaining any defiled thoughts. Keep the body clean too. Do not indulge in doing any tainted practices. Always maintain purity and avoid the slightest misbehavior.

Reciting the Shurangama Mantra is more profitable than trading in gold. One recitation of the Shurangama Mantra is as valuable as several billion ounces of gold. But do not recite out of greed. If we can uphold the precepts; if we can be free of jealousy and obstructions; if we can be free of greed, hatred and delusion; then we will reap huge responses and benefit from reciting the Shurangama Mantra. If we misbehave while cultivating this Dharma, then the power of response will not be nearly as great. It is not that this mantra is ineffective but that we misbehave; as a result, the Dharma protecting good spirits stay far away from us. They will not bother with anything that happens to us.

Anyone who reads and recites the Shurangama Mantra must not be treacherous and must not commit offenses repeatedly. Always be proper and bright at all times so that we only know about benefiting others and not about benefiting ourselves, practicing the ways of the Bodhisattvas with the heart of Bodhisattvas.

Uphold the Precepts, Cultivate Samadhi, and Wisdom will Unfold

We can cause our offenses to melt away by reciting the Shurangama Mantra.

Originally there was no way to make up for having broken some precepts, but by reciting the Shurangama Mantra, we may restore the purity in our precepts. Of course that does not entail just reciting it, it means we recite it to the point that we reach samadhi. This mantra comes from our mind and can come back into our mind. The mantra heart and the heart of the mantra—the heart and the mantra unite as one. There are no longer distinctions. Even if we want to forget it, we cannot. This is reciting but not reciting, reciting without reciting.

Recite so that all false and random thoughts vanish. The

only thought we have is that of reciting the Shurangama Mantra. All other thoughts fuse with that thought and become one. Our thoughts unite so that we do not have a second thought. That continuous thought acts like flowing water, with one wave pushing the one before it. "The water flows and the wind blows at the shore of Mahayana." The sounds of flowing water and wafting breeze are the heart of the mantra. Were we to be able to recite like this and were we to have broken the precepts, they would be restored to a state of purity. We would receive precepts that we have not yet received formally. Even if we did not want to make progress in our studies of the Buddhadharma, after reciting the Shurangama Mantra for a while, we will naturally become diligent. Someone who lacked wisdom will uncover his or her wisdom.

By not forgetting the Shurangama Mantra, we will quickly restore our purity tainted by violating the rules for eating or other precepts. If we had violated prohibitive precepts before we started to practice this mantra or received the precepts, then regardless of the seriousness of the offense, the offense will be eliminated because we recite the Shurangama Mantra. Such offenses include violation of any rule related to eating, violation of major and minor precepts, even violation of any of the four parajikas, for which no repentance is possible, violation of the five rebellious acts, and violation of the eight parajikas. Not one single bit of offense will remain. That is because the power of the Shurangama Mantra is inconceivable.

Some people hear about the effectiveness of the Shurangama Mantra and so they do not cultivate but only recite the mantra. That kind of behavior is too extreme. No matter which Dharma we practice, we want to keep to the Middle Way, not being excessive or deficient. Although this mantra is effective, we must also cultivate Samadhi. The Shurangama Sutra talks about the effectiveness of this mantra as well as the practice of turning back our hearing to listen to our inherent nature; the perfection of the ear organ is also critical.

While we recite the mantra, we should also return our hearing to listen to our inherent nature. Turn our light inward and reflect. Did we not say earlier that this mantra is the mind and the mind is this mantra? The mind and this mantra are inseparable. The mind and mantra are two and yet not two. Having reached this state, we will get whatever we want. We will succeed for sure. When the mind and the mantra come together, we will have reached the Samadhi of chan, the real power of Samadhi. This is one point that each of us must know.

PART TWO - RECORDS

OF MIRACLES RELATED
TO THE I
SHURANGAMA MANTRA

The Shurangama Mantra
Rescued Me

When I concentrated on reciting the Shurangama Mantra, difficulties dissolved quickly.

by Gwo Lan

Since I started to study Buddhism at the age of 30, I met with some very helpful conditions. Once while shopping at a frame shop, I noticed a frame containing Great Master Yinguang's excellent instructions: "Whether at home or left home, we must pay respects to those above and interact harmoniously with those below; bear what people cannot bear; do what other people cannot do; help others with their work; and help others reach their success. Sit quietly and always reflect on our faults. We do not discuss the mistakes of others. While walking, standing, sitting and resting, dressing and eating from morning to night, from night to morning, continue unceasingly with the Buddha's name.

Recite quietly or silently. Have no other thought besides the Buddha's name. Or if a false thought occurs, extinguish it right away. Always be ashamed and repentant. Even if we have some level of cultivation, always consider our skills shallow and do not brag. Watch only ourselves and do not bother checking others. Only see other people's strengths and not their faults. See everyone else as a Bodhisattva, but we as ordinary people. Those who do as I say will definitely become born in the Western Land of Ultimate Bliss."

I was delighted the instant I read this passage. I borrowed it from the shop owner and made a copy. I asked someone to write it out and then I had it framed. I hung it in the middle of our staircase. I read it several dozen times a day as I went up and down the stairs everyday. This is how I impressed Great Master Yinguang's "While walking, standing, sitting and resting, dressing and eating from morning to night, from night to morning, continue uninterruptedly with the Buddha's name" deep into my mind. I devotedly applied it and integrated the Buddha's name completely into my daily life, reciting the Buddha's name once per movement.

Having developed a bit of concentration from reciting Amitabha Buddha's name uninterruptedly wile eating, dressing, dwelling and walking, I felt more and more abnormal. Often times, what I utter was not what I intended. I often encountered things that went against my wishes while my mood swung high and low. I felt so wronged because what I did was not what I did was not what I did was not what I intended; people misunderstood me. Gradually I noticed that I had another voice in my head. I was being controlled by this voice.

As I think back on the times when I was in elementary school, one night around seven or eight o'clok, I was doing homework at home, which was located in the countryside. A shadow appeared on the see-through glass door, he smirked with his two white teeth showing, "Hee, hee!" Now that I think back I realized that he was telling me, "Hey, hey, hey, I finally found you." The next two consecutive nights, a green face appeared inside my blanket. No matter how I shut my eyes or hid inside the blanket, I kept seeing his green face and how he was staring at me with his big, wide-open eyes. He vanished as I became extremely scared. But since then, misfortune also followed me; I seemed to be walking down a path of frustration everywhere I went. Many obstructions followed me. I was always misunderstood, wrongly accused and once even attacked by a mob sometimes. These adversities reduced when I was nearing the edge of a breakdown. One difficulty after another came at me from every direction. I was left with a profound sense of how we suffer in the world. Once I nearly went insane and after an episode that nearly caused me a concussion of the brain, I fell at the feet of Guanshiyin Bodhisattva, crying and praying for Guanshiyin to point out a reputable teacher who will teach me how to cultivate. Consequently I learned about the Venerable Master and by chance acquired a volume of Venerable Master Hsuan Hua's talks. I had obtained a most valuable treasure.

I finished the book on the talks as if in a single breath. I did not want to eat or sleep. After experiencing a few days in the joy of Dharma, I tried to get the entire series of the Master's talks, explanations of sutras, and every issue of "The Source of Wisdom." I spent half a year studying them in depth. "The Meaning of Life" contained one article about the Venerable Master propagating the Dharma in Taiwan. The reporters interviewed the Venerable Master on how he converted those free and liberal young people in the West who are quite difficult to tame. The Venerable Master answered, "With the Shurangama Mantra, Great Compassion Mantra and Guanshiyin Bodhisattva."

I always thought, if this is what a great teacher does, then an ordinary individual like me must do at least that much. So from then on, I have been doing the Shurangama Mantra and Great Compassion Mantra as a practice, especially the Shurangama Mantra. My first action at work every day is to play the Shurangama Mantra. I spend more than a dozen hours in the day permeated in the recitation of the Shurangama Mantra. Everyday during break, I would sit down and recite the Shurangama Mantra out of a booklet. What was incredible was that when I concentrated on reciting the Shurangama Mantra, difficulties dissolved quickly. I finally understood what was meant by turning afflictions into Bodhi. When afflictions occur, recite the Shurangama Mantra calmly and afflictions soon cease. The Shurangama Mantra is like a sharp knife that can cut away all anger, ignorance and afflictions.

The Venerable Master always said, "Always turn our light inward and reflect, seek for the answers within. Do not pursue things outside." When afflictions and ignorance arise, be ashamed and repent instantly. Always feel that we are at fault. When a conflict arises, always resolve it with gratitude. From where do afflictions come? From where will ignorance arise? These are all created from our one thought. When thoughts turn toward what is good, all unpleasantness disappears. When conflicts occur in my life or in my business, I think about what the Venerable Master said, "Give others what they want. We pick up what others do not want." What is there to fight over? Cultivation is about becoming liberated from the cycle of birth and death and about benefiting all beings. In the process of becoming Bodhisattvas or Buddhas, we do not ever leave sentient beings.

I am very grateful to have met such fine Buddhadharma and an excellent teacher; they are a bright lamp for me to follow on the way to Buddhahood. During the two years that I recited the Shurangama Mantra, I really felt the tremendous power of the Shurangama Mantra. I would be turned by situations if I were just slightly lazy. I would be clear about situations if I were diligent in my cultivation. While walking, standing, sitting or resting, I always told myself that I will become a Bodhisattva; I do not want to be an ordinary individual. Ordinary people are swayed by states, while Bodhisattvas can change states. The Master's instructions always ring in my ear: "In the Shurangama Samadhi, one can be just as one is, unmoving and enjoying clear understanding all the time. One is not swayed by states but changes all states. Without the Shurangama Samadhi, one is swayed by states. One pursues whatever states come, being swayed by them."

Looking back at that miserable period of time in my life when I was not in control of myself, I felt like I was a puppet that lived in so much pain. That feeling was the polar opposite of the feeling that I now enjoy because I recite the Shurangama Mantra. Always use joy, gratitude, a sense of shame, and penitence in facing any situation peacefully. End past karma according to conditions. No one gave us any afflictions. When the mind opens up, situations open themselves up. All karma is made from the mind alone. Karma dies when the mind quits making it.

I am ashamed and penitent because of my resentment, which had been created out of ignorance in my past lives. Do no evil and devote to doing all good. When virtues are great, enmity and offenses vanish. I always warn myself, a Bodhisattva is afraid of causes while ordinary beings are afraid of consequences. Make no mistakes in terms of cause and effect, that way we avoid being untrue at the stage of planting causes and avoid having to face warped results.

I wrote this article today because I wish to share all the advantages that I had gained from the Shurangama Mantra. I hope everyone will also reap advantages from the Shurangama Mantra.

Recite the Shurangama Mantra and Develop Great Wisdom

People who recite the Shurangama Mantra cannot be harmed by poison.

by Bhikshuni Heng Jhuang

In celebration of the Venerable Master's birthday, we are having a Shurangama Mantra Dharma Assembly this week. The Venerable Master is very compassionate and hopes that his disciples will recite the Shurangama Mantra and study the Shurangama Sutra. We beings in the Saha World experience numerous afflictions and yet we do not realize that we are suffering. We think we are very happy. This is why Buddhas and Bodhisattvas have revealed this expedient practice, the Shurangama Sutra, to guide us out of suffering so we can attain bliss.

The Shurangama Mantra was spoken because of the Venerable Ananda. He nearly fell when he encountered Matangi's daughter and the former Brahma Heaven mantra, the Kapila mantra. Shakyamuni Buddha told Manjushri Bodhisattva to save Ananda with the Shurangama Mantra. The Shurangama Sutra explains the advantages of the Shurangama Mantra and teaches us the sequence to cultivation. The Master told us that if we uphold the Shurangama Mantra then we can fight King Yama. When I first entered the Buddhist Academy, one Dharma Master told the class, "The Sutra on the Ultimate Meaning That Has Been Cultivated and Certified to by means of the Thus Come One's Secret Cause at the Crown of the Great Buddha is the Foremost Among the Myriad Practices of Every Bodhisattva—the principles in that sutra—make all things firm and solid ultimately."

The Dharma Master explained this several times and I never understood. What does it mean by ultimately firm and solid? After half a year, I gradually came to understand it more. The meaning of ultimately firm and solid says that we can uncover great wisdom by reciting the Shurangama Mantra. What is great wisdom? Wisdom is Samadhi. When afflictions come, we develop wisdom, coming up with wonderful dharmas that counter our afflictions so that we are not turned by external distresses, hence "firm and solid." After upholding the Shurangama Mantra as a practice for a long time, we will attain truly firm and solid strength.

The great Shurangama Samadhi exists everywhere and at all times. No matter when and where, it is ultimately firm and solid.

We do not uphold the Shurangama Mantra in the monastery only. We also uphold the Shurangama Mantra on a regular basis. Laypeople are often quite busy, but they can use their free time to keep reciting so that they become quite familiar with it. Eventually, they are so familiar with it that they can uphold the Shurangama Mantra all the time, whether working, walking, riding in the car or even on a motorcycle. Suppose we were going somewhere and suddenly something happens that is going to prevent us from reaching our destination, and so we become distressed. If we ordinarily recite the Shurangama Mantra, we will be relaxed despite the delay. We acquire great wisdom from upholding the Shurangama Mantra. When things do not go as we wish, we let it go. At the same time, the sutras say that people who uphold the Shurangama Mantra will be wealthy for seven lives; but those of us who study the Buddhadharma do not pray to become rich. We pray for transcendental wealth that allows us to become liberated from birth and death. That kind of wisdom is real wealth.

To cultivate the great Shurangama Samadhi, we must first stop killing; second, stop stealing; third, stop sexual misconduct; fourth, stop lying. These four clear instructions on purity are most important and everyone knows, but the

Venerable Master tells us we must cultivate to transcend the Desire Realm, the Form Realm, and the Formless Realm. Desire includes a lot. For example, it applies to food or wanting fine clothes or nice lodging. These various pleasures are included in the category of desire. Desire distresses us. When we continue to roll about in desire, we cannot pull ourselves out. How do we leave the Desire Realm? We must uphold the Shurangama Mantra, which eliminates desire. When we reach Samadhi, we are not swayed by the six kinds of objects. The six senses create the karma of birth and death. The six senses are eyes, ears, nose, tongue, body and mind. Our false thinking creates a wish for something, so we take action.

We can calm our mind by reciting the Shurangama Mantra, hence refusing to see form and refusing to eat delicious foods. The Shurangama Mantra is the mind to mind imprint of all Buddhas. It is the prince of the great Dharma.

It can make us leave birth and escape fear. The purpose of studying Buddhism is to find this mind of ours. Where exactly is our mind? When we recite the Shurangama Mantra long enough then we will quite naturally one day, find the mind and perceive what the Buddha nature is like. It is very pure and very bright, like a lotus blossom. A lotus is not tainted though it grows up through mud. It remains quite pure. Similarly, we are in this evil world of the five turbidities and cannot escape it, so we can only recite the Shurangama Mantra. People who recite the Shurangama Mantra cannot be harmed by any poison. Since the Shurangama Mantra is very long, if we cannot memorize it, we can wear it or place it on our altar at home for worship and offerings. This way, no poison can harm us. The Mantra can even control all demons and heretics. All Buddhas and Bodhisattvas throughout the ten directions protect and are mindful of the Shurangama Mantra. If we recite sincerely then we will naturally be blessed and aided by all Buddhas, Bodhisattvas, dragons and gods.

Recite the Shurangama Mantra
to Stay Far Away
from Evil Dharmas

There is more and more chaos, more and more disturbing phenomena, which further prove the importance of the Shurangama Sutra and the Shurangama Mantra.

by Gwo Qiang Yang

When I was 18 (1987), my father suddenly passed away because of a stroke. That was a major shock in my life. My father was someone who never got angry and was willing to take losses in any situation. I wanted to emulate my father in spirit, so I took refuge with Buddhism and started to come into contact with the Buddhadharma.

I could never find a good teacher in Taiwan, so I spent a blurry two years in Buddhism. During this period of time, I saw some signs of the Dharma on its decline and that made me become skeptical about Buddhism. Because of my studies, I rented a place above a Buddhist book store in 1989. The landlord invited a layperson to teach the Buddhadharma when I was living upstairs. I was invited to participate.

Of the more than 20 Dharma brothers who participated, all gradually had miraculous responses, including what they called "opening heavenly eyes." (In their cases, it was actually just connecting with the ghosts). Perhaps they started dancing or doing martial arts for no reason. Only another layman and I had no reactions. I even thought his theories were strange (once I began to recite the Shurangama Mantra). But we read very few sutras and did not have enough knowledge to name the problem.

Later the layman from the United States told us that we do not necessarily have to be vegetarians to cultivate. It does not even matter that we eat meat. He also told some people privately, "I have a certain pure land in the heaven. You are my concubines, wives, Dharma protectors in the heavens. I came to rescue you to take you back to the heavens." I really did not know what to do then, so I prayed to Guanshiyin Bodhisattva: let me have wisdom to tell the difference between that which is evil and proper. I started looking for answers in many of the thousands of Buddhist texts in the book store. The first book I opened was an explanation of the 50 skandha demons. The commentator was the

Venerable Master Hsuan Hua. I was very happy to have proved that my view was correct and that the layman's idea that eating meat is acceptable goes against the Shurangama's four kinds of clear instructions on purity. The theory of "having a certain pure land in the heavens" is just a 50 skandha demon phenomenon.

When I saw the guidelines the Venerable Master established, which are: "freezing to death we do not scheme, starving to death we do not beg, dying of poverty we ask for nothing." I realized then that the strange phenomena I saw in Buddhism in the past were created by people. At one end of the earth though, there was an old monk and his disciples who worked hard to continue the Buddha's proper Dharma. Especially the Venerable Master's spirit of self-sacrifice: "As long as I am present, the Dharma is forbidden to end." His justness and altruism moved me deeply. He had huge vows to suffer on behalf of all beings. Suddenly my doubts about Buddhism cleared up. In addition, I found a master who really had gall and cultivation. I took refuge with the Venerable Master when he came to Taiwan to propagate the Dharma in 1990. I selected the Venerable Master as my good and wise teacher for the rest of my life and received the five precepts.

During the time when the Dharma is on its decline, there is more and more chaos, more and more disturbing phenomena, which further prove the importance of the Shurangama Sutra and the Shurangama Mantra. I have been reciting the Shurangama Mantra continuously these several years. I hope that everyone will recite the Shurangama Mantra and become very familiar the Shurangama Sutra. Besides the fact that it gives me the ability to differentiate between what is proper and evil; more importantly, it will continue the will and wish of the Venerable Master so that the Proper Dharma lasts.

A Peaceful Mind

At the same time, a golden strand of Shurangama Mantra appeared before me like it was real.

by Mei Hua Tan

Ever since young, I was always frightened. Often times I did not dare to stay home alone. Before I came into contact with the Buddhadharma, I was often troubled by a ghost that pressed me down. My sleep always began with a series of nightmares. These phenomena became more serious in China. The whole family suffered with me. Things only took a turn for the better when I met my now good friend Xuanfa Wang.

Having studied Buddhism for a long time, she sent me a little Shurangama Mantra to wear around my neck that she had gotten from one of the Venerable Master Hsuan Hua's monasteries. I wore it every day. I only took it off when I bathed. She also sent me a framed Great Compassion Dharani Mantra. I hung it at the end of my bed. Strangely enough, the problem of being pressed down by ghosts greatly improved. Later, I added being a vegetarian ten days out of the month so that my outlook gradually improved.

But then, even more bizarre was that while I was taking a nap at work, I was again pressed down by a strong force all of a sudden so that I could not breath. Though in a panic, I knew that I was being pressed down by a ghost again.

Waves of fear attacked me so that I did not know what to do. I was in such torment and fright that I could not concentrate and finish the entire Heart Sutra. My incomplete recitation did not work. I was like a popped balloon, powerless over what to do. Just as I was ready to give up, a bright idea flashed across my mind. Quicker than I could speak, an image of that Shurangama Mantra which I wore around my neck flashed into my head. At the same time, a golden strand of Shurangama Mantra appeared before me like it was real. Suddenly, that heavy load on my body vanished. My misery came to an end.

How could this series of incidents that I experienced be so mystical unless they were due to the power of the Buddhadharma? I, at least, have absolutely no doubt about it. Being a vegetarian and reciting the Buddha's name and reciting sutras on a regular basis ensures my peace. Only those who have had similar experiences understand.

A Response from
the Shurangama Mantra

While reciting the Shurangama Mantra, a white light appeared and separated the ghost and myself.

by Xuangfa Wang

During 1995's Chinese New Year I went to my husband's grandmother's place in Gaoxiong, Taiwan. Since my grandfather was an admiral in the Navy, he was assigned a large residence that included lodging for orderlies too. When my husband and I went there, we stayed in the rooms normally assigned to orderlies.

After five o'clock in the evening on New Year's day, I was alone in the room preparing to do the evening ceremony. When I just started the incense praise, I felt a chill on my scalp that made me numb. I had been pestered by ghosts before and knew this was the same situation. So

I concentrated on reciting the Shurangama Mantra. I recited loudly "Namo Sadanduo, suqieduoye, alahedi, sanmiaosanputuoxie, namosadanduo . . ."When I got to this line, I felt something warm going from the top of my head to the bottom of my feet. I was all of a sudden no longer cold and my scalp was no longer numb. I knew that the Buddhas and Bodhisattvas were aiding me. My gratitude was indescribable and I even dared to turn out the lights and sleep that night.

When I went to Gaoxiong in 1994, I had just started learning about Buddhism and was not reciting sutras or mantras so I used to get so scared that I kept the brightest lights on. I could not get any shut-eye. Fortunately I had the great compassion mantra and rebirth mantra CDs with me. I wore my headphones until dawn. There was another response that came in a dream because I recited the mantra. I had dreamt that I was being chased by a male ghost whose face was burnt. He looked vicious. While reciting the Shurangama Mantra, a white light appeared and separated the ghost and myself.

In another dream I was stuck in a courtyard. It was really dark and the courtyard was haunted. By the time I recited to the third assembly of the Shurangama Mantra, the sun was up. I was able to walk out of the courtyard and get ready to ride back home. Lastly, I dreamt of holding hands with a little girl and knew that we were mother and daughter.

When I woke up, I prayed to the Buddhas to have this little girl become born elsewhere because I wanted to cultivate and did not want to give birth. For the next consecutive week, I recited the Shurangama Sutra and mantra, dedicating the merit to that little girl. A week later, I dreamt of that little girl becoming transparent and vanishing.

I believe what the Shurangama Sutra says about the Shurangama Mantra, which is incredible. I set up a regular schedule for reciting the Shurangama Mantra and bowing to the Avatamsaka Sutra every day. I hope that the Buddhas and Bodhisattvas will bless me and make my resolve firm, diligently work on eliminating the habits of ignorance in my eighth consciousness so that I will realize Buddhahood soon.

Collecting Resources by Reciting the Shurangama Mantra

Reciting the Shurangama Mantra, all the layers of shadows in my body and mind were wiped away.

by Zhaoli Chen

I took refuge with Venerable Hua in 1993. When Venerable Master Hsuan Hua arrived in Taiwan on January 17, 1993, the entire sports stadiums was packed. Everyone recited the Shurangama Mantra during each day of the Dharma Assembly. It was very difficult for a beginner like me. My tongue did not follow my orders and did not work smoothly. I did not know the mantra and had no firm commitment to learning it. Whenever I picked up the book, lethargy would interfere so that I could not concentrate; I was restless, jumpy and perturbed. I certainly cannot say that I was cultivating diligently. I recited the mantra on and off during one year and saw very little result.

Everyone praises the Shurangama Mantra for being the king among mantras. Recite it and one's past obstructions are completely eliminated. I received no response at all and made slow progress. Things work whenever we concentrate. I took the opportunity to participate in a week of Shurangama session and several consecutive sessions of reciting the Buddha's name. I learned a little bit about reciting the Shurangama Mantra from cultivating with a group. There are many lines in the mantra that are repetitive or complicated, that is why it is hard to recite. As one adage goes, practice makes perfect. Now I read it three times every morning and it takes about 28 minutes. After reading it I feel clearheaded, as if I had been given a strong shot that clears away thoughts and reduces desires. Sometimes when I am in a bad mood, the Shurangama Mantra is like a clear spring of sweetness that washes away heated afflictions. Over time my faith became stronger, everything seems perfect and problem-free. I am always so happy.

What motivated me to consistently recite was that most unbearable day, December 23, 1986. My husband had lung cancer and could not be saved in the care of Taiwan General Hospital's emergency team. At that instant, I was as if struck by a bolt from the blue. I was shocked and in a panic. Pressured by every possible feeling of misery, I looked up helplessly and asked the Buddhas and Bodhisattvas: what do I do now? At that moment, a pure light of gold flashed before my eyes. In my surprise, I suddenly remembered the king among mantras. I immediately told my children to prepare to recite the Shurangama Mantra and chant Amitabha Buddha's name. We recited them continuously during all hours of the day. My husband did not suffer but headed for rebirth in the Land of Ultimate Bliss in peace.

An adage goes, "one individual becomes enlightened and his nine types of relatives will become born in the heavens." From my having received the Bodhisattva precepts, being a vegetarian, reciting the Shurangama Mantra and reading the sutras, my entire family benefited a great deal. I had been especially fortunate because I came in contact with this most pure and beneficial Dharma. All the distresses and habits were swept away. I revel in joy every day. Reciting the Shurangama Mantra, all the layers of shadows in my body and mind were wiped away. My long-time companion has passed away and I live alone as an old woman. I pass my time by reciting the sutras and mantras every day. My days are pleasant. A calm mind is blessed; contentment is joy. I am at peace because I can be patient. Wherever there is no seeking, there are no worries.

I want to give up my bad habits from the past and try to cultivate blessings and wisdom. I learned that I myself must study hard for a long time, and must be sincere and honest. Basically, the unsurpassed treasury is in my mind. Now I have to excavate it. I, Gwo Li, had taken refuge with the Triple Jewel with a singleness of mind. May I be bold and diligent, never give up or be lazy. May I be persistent and out of the 84,000 different practices, select a practice that suits me. The Shurangama Mantra is simple but profound and contains limitless meanings. It plants seeds of purity in the mind-field of Buddhas. I hope to intently and diligently irrigate my mind-field so that when I harvest an abundance of fruits I will then share them. The Shurangama Mantra is a treasury that cannot be emptied or exhausted. The more it gets excavated, the shinier it becomes. May all greatly virtuous ones dig in and find it too!

During the Decline of Dharma, Everyone Should Memorize the Shurangama Mantra Well

All those who believe they are orthodox Buddhists should make the huge resolve to recite the Shurangama Mantra for the entire world.

by Gwo Zheng Xie

The Master says, "When the Shurangama flourishes, the Buddhadharma flourishes; when the Shurangama extinguishes, the Buddhadharma extinguishes." All those who believe they are orthodox Buddhists should make the huge resolve to recite the Shurangama Mantra for the entire world so that a righteous, proper energy endures and the orthodox Dharma lives on forever. This is the kind of attitude that contemporary Buddhists should have toward studying Buddhism.

Since having taken refuge with the Master in 1990, I heard

tapes of the Master's instructions that say that he had been able to propagate the Dharma in the West primarily because of the power of the Shurangama Mantra and the Great Compassion Mantra. The power of these two mantras made him deeply enter what was originally a Buddhist "desert", societies of countries in the West where non-Buddhism is prevalent. He achieved sacred Buddhist work that will endure and prosper for thousands upon thousands of generations.

In 1968 the Master began to propagate the Dharma for Westerners in San Francisco, U.S. He started by explaining the Shurangama Sutra (which includes the Shurangama Mantra). From this we can tell how important and urgent the Shurangama Sutra and the Shurangama Mantra are when it comes to inspiring and lifting people's morale—in ways that other Buddhist sutras cannot compare. In other words, the Shurangama Sutra and the Shurangama Mantra are most suitable for this time and age when people are preoccupied with lust and when moral ethics is nearly in ruins. This is also the best Dharma jewel because it provides a strong warning. During the age when Dharma is in its decline, demonic energy is strong and the proper energy is weak. Demons and ghosts are making waves everywhere so that people are corrupt and the world is not peaceful. The average people with their average vision cannot tell the difference between demons and ghosts; those who have opened their five spiritual eyes and who can use some of the six spiritual powers are exceptions. Ghosts and goblins are especially afraid of the Shurangama Sutra and the Shurangama Mantra. The principles in the Shurangama Sutra are so true and the power of the Shurangama Mantra is so mighty that when we recite the Shurangama Mantra, various cults and sects are instilled with real fear and are forced to become well-behaved, not daring to be wanton. The Venerable Master said, "The Mantra's power is tremendous, pervading all of space and the Dharma Realm so that there is no place devoid of this peaceful light and auspicious energy. That is why the recitations of the Shurangama Mantra can make up for the lack of healthy energy in the universe."

At the gate of the City of Ten Thousand Buddhas in California, U.S.A., is a couplet the Master composed. The right side of the couplet says, "Flower Adornment Dharma Assembly, Shurangama Platform, and 42 Hands and Eyes Peacefully Establish Heaven and Earth." From this we can tell that the Master mostly relied on the Avatamsaka Sutra, the Shurangama Sutra and Mantra, and the 42 Hands and Eyes of the Great Compassion Mantra to settle heaven and earth in peace, quietly using the power of the Buddhadharma for seeking world peace. The Master especially praised the Shurangama Sutra and Mantra. He also continuously urged that Buddhists during this Dharma-Ending Age become familiar with the Shurangama Sutra and recite the Shurangama Mantra by heart. Only then will they be qualified to be "real Buddhists." He had said, "The Shurangama Mantra has to do with the flourishing and decline of all of Buddhism. It is the magical text that sustains the world and keeps it from being doomed. As long as one individual knows how to read the Shurangama Mantra, this world will not be destroyed."

The Shurangama Sutra makes it quite clear: as long as we can uphold and recite the Shurangama Mantra, then all kinds of disasters, including famine, plague, warfare and robberies turn into fortune. All your prayers will be answered. It works especially well.

I recall in 1994 when I was working in Los Angeles, U.S., I was driving my two 13-year-old nieces to Long Beach Monastery for a Dharma Assembly. On the way, these two little devils were playing around in the backseat and would not listen to me. I was at the end of my tethers so I thought I might as well not bother with them. I played a tape of the Shurangama Mantra that I had recorded at the City of 10,000 Buddhas and recited along for five or six minutes. Suddenly I sensed that it was silent in the back. I looked in the rearview mirror and saw the two of them had their eyes closed and were leaning against the seat of the car, looking like two stiff worms. I thought, "Is it the power of the Shurangama Mantra that chased away the 'naughty ghosts' on them in these few short minutes?" This is the first time and by accident that I felt the wondrousness of the

Shurangama Mantra.

The Venerable Master had instructed that the wonderful uses and merit from reciting the Shurangama Mantra are incredible and incapable of being described completely even until the end of the future. "Everything that is said in the Shurangama Mantra tames heavenly demons and heretics. From start to finish, its every line is a Dharma about the mind-ground of all Buddhas. Each line has its use and each syllable has its wondrousness, all of which contains inconceivable power. Reciting one syllable, one line, one section or the entire mantra will rock the universe, or as it is said, "Startle heaven and earth and move ghosts and spirits to tears. Monsters and demons stay far away and ghosts and goblins hide." Later I developed the habit of reciting the Shurangama Mantra while driving so that I felt like my car was imperceptibly filled with the Shurangama Mantra. Over time I noticed that all of my passengers either become quieter (though they may be verbose usually) or fall asleep readily. I believe this is also the power the Shurangama Mantra quietly at work!

Another thing that is worth mentioning has to do with my parents. Ever since young, I watched them fight. After some hard work on my part, they became vegetarians. But my father's garrulous and hot temper did not improve. Conversely, it expanded and intensified with age. I could never figure it out because I had heard that being vegetarian makes people mellower. But this did not happen to him. Perhaps this is a sickness common to many elders or that he has heavy karmic obstructions so that "ghosts of anger" frequently make him act up. In short, I felt awful about being caught between my parents and their bickering.

Having learned the Shurangama Mantra by heart, I thought about trying it out. The Master had said, "Reciting the Shurangama Mantra frequently helps eliminate our karmic obstructions and offenses from our past lives." "Whether it is major or minor, even the unrepentable four parajikas, five rebellious acts, eight parajikas, just recite the Shurangama Mantra and whatever serious offenses we have incurred vanish, leaving not even a hair's worth." This means that reciting the Shurangama Mantra is one of the fastest and most thorough practices to eliminate karmic obstructions. I dedicated the merit I gained from reciting the Shurangama Mantra while commuting to and from work to these two elders. I wished for them to be less angry. I did see improvement relatively quickly; they argued less, for example. Sometimes when I walked into the door and see my father sitting home alone in front of the television, I see that he is like a compliant "lamb". It seemed as if he could not raise his fire of ignorance even if he wanted to. It is as if the Vajra Treasury Bodhisattvas or ghosts or spirit kings in the Shurangama Mantra had steadied and tamed the "ghost of anger" possessing him. It did not dare to misbehave. Of course, I also understood that unless he personally wished to study Buddhism and really cultivate, the power of the Shurangama Mantra is external to him and can only improve but not cut off the source of his bad temper.

I also tried to repent to eliminate his karmic obstructions and hope that one day he will enlighten to his inherent nature and start to study Buddhism. However, up to this point my virtuous practices have not been able to change him enough for him to take refuge with Buddhism. I hope that all Buddhas and Bodhisattvas will bless him so that he will take refuge soon, cultivate sincerely and change his bad temper. If this is made possible, I will be so happy because my life will not have been a waste.

The Venerable Master said, "It is best for people who uphold and recite the Shurangama Mantra to make the great resolve to recite for the entire world, dedicating such merit to the entire world." One of the Master's eighteen great vows is "May all beings who see me or even hear my name bring forth their resolve for Bodhi and realize Buddhahood soon." How vast is this vow! I am also emulating the Venerable Master now and reciting the Shurangama Mantra everyday and dedicating such merit to not only my parents or friends and family, but to all of my coworkers and their families, everyone I meet or call that day and even all sentient and insentient beings throughout the Dharma Realm. May they realize Buddhahood soon. Having started doing this, I felt that a good amount of friction in dealing with people has dissolved. Sometimes things are done much more efficiently and make a positive impact. It would be hard for me to quit reciting the Shurangama Mantra even for a day because I have already integrated it into my life. I try my best to apply it to every facet of my life. I am gradually getting a sense of its wonderful uses. Here, I would also like to make the vow that I will support and recite the Shurangama Mantra so that the proper Dharma lasts and the world becomes a better place.

One of the most conspicuous features of upholding the Shurangama Mantra is that the merit that goes to the practitioner is supreme. The Venerable Master had said that if we can memorize the Shurangama Mantra by heart so that our recitation is like flowing water, continuous and nonstop, then we would have reached the Samadhi of upholding the mantra. At the minimum, we will, for seven lives, be as rich as the wealthiest of people, such as the American oil magnates. Although people can acquire such excellent blessings from reciting the Shurangama Mantra, I want to remind everyone not to be small-minded. Seven lives as a rich person go by in a blink of an eye. So what should we hope for by reciting the Shurangama Mantra? We should hope to become Buddhas ultimately, reaching the Unsurpassed, Proper, Equal and Right Enlightenment. We are actually transformations of Buddhas because we study the Shurangama Mantra. Not only are we transformations of Buddhas, but a transformational Buddha from the top of the Buddha's head. If we accept and uphold the Shurangama Mantra, we will definitely become a Buddha in the future. This is the guarantee that the Master had promised us.

This is also a practice that is difficult to encounter in billions and billions of eons. The City of 10,000 Buddhas is probably the only place in the world of Buddhism that can thoroughly explain the principles and wonderful uses of the Shurangama Mantra. Since the Shurangama Mantra is critical to all of Buddhism and the fate of the world, how could a Buddhist not seriously treasure it, support it and share its principles on a vast scale?

Since results that come from reciting the Shurangama Mantra are especially efficacious and swift, its power and merit are tremendous as well. Hence the practitioner must have a pure mind, be bright and just in speech and behavior, and adhere to the precepts so that he will be successful. Just as the Master said, we should, at the least, observe the Five Precepts and devote ourselves to doing ten kinds of good acts. Otherwise not only will we not receive any results, we will attract problems. Some people hear this and do not dare to study the Shurangama Mantra. Actually Buddhists should already be observing the precepts. Filled with greed, hatred and delusion, we will fail in any endeavor despite the fact that we recite sutras or mantras. Sometimes minor problems serve as a kind of warning or test that make us collect our thoughts, follow the rules and not violate the precepts again.

Having gone back to Taiwan to work, I had an opportunity to introduce the wonderful aspects of upholding the Shurangama Mantra to coworkers who have affinities with it. I often get this response from them: "I heard that we can only recite the Shurangama Mantra in the morning and not other times; otherwise it will be hurtful." How many masters in Taiwan's monasteries teach people to recite the Shurangama Mantra only during the morning and avoid it like the plague during other hours of the day? The Buddha is compassionate and impartial; he is not prejudiced against this mantra. Just consider this false information.

Demons and heretics and their followings created this kind of rumor to destroy the Shurangama Mantra, of which they are most afraid. They hope that people will recite this mantra less so that they may prevail and perpetrate evil, committing more mischief in the world. The Buddha also said that in the Age of the Decline of Dharma, the first Buddhadharma to perish are the Shurangama Sutra and Mantra. Demon kings and their retinues wish to destroy this sutra and mantra most desperately, and they make every attempt to do so. Many ignorant teachers follow the baton of demons and avoid the Shurangama Sutra and Mantra as much as possible. I have friends who have studied Buddhism for more than a dozen years but have never heard of the Shurangama Mantra. This is a major loss and regret for Buddhism.

Someone asked the Venerable Master Hsuan Hua, "I heard we can recite the Shurangama Mantra at five a.m. but not other times." The Venerable Master said, "Recite it any time. Any time is five a.m. Morning here is night in the United States. So how do you figure? Do not be attached to appearances when reciting the sutras and mantras. Recite at any time and results will occur at any time." How fortunate for us to have such guidance from a great teacher like Venerable Master Hsuan Hua! His words are like the evening drums and morning bells, waking up many teachers who had been misled.

The Venerable Master said, "When the Shurangama flourishes, the Buddhadharma flourishes. When the Shurangama is gone, the Buddhadharma will go." During this time and age, moral values and ethical considerations are eroding. Not only Taiwan, the entire world has reached a perilous moment when we are face to face with birth and death, survival and demise, extinction and continuation. All those who believe they are orthodox Buddhists should make the huge resolve to recite the Shurangama Mantra all the time for the whole world. That way we can roll back the tides of an impending disaster, allow wholesome and just energy to prevail, and keep the proper Dharma alive. This is the attitude contemporary Buddhists should have toward studying Buddhism.

The Start of a New Life

> *If we sincerely concentrate on reciting the magical Shurangama Mantra, why worry that we will not reaize our inherent nature and become Buddhas?*
>
> *by Gwo Chang*

We should not be attached to results as we study Buddhism. But "the Buddhas grant miracles to people who are sincere." If our thoughts are pure to start with, working hard on our cultivation without wishing for rewards, then we will get the responses we want even if we do not ask for them. Otherwise, we would be trapped in the situation of "being untrue at the start and ending up with warped results." I am grateful for the Shurangama Mantra. Although I read the Shurangama Mantra with ordinary and even unrefined thoughts, perhaps because of a trace of sincerity and respect, I have enjoyed some results in a couple of months. This is something I had never expected at the start.

How did I come to have the opportunity to accept and uphold the Shurangama Mantra? The Venerable Master should get the credit for this. He tried his hardest to encourage us to enter the treasury of sutra deeply so that we may have wisdom like the sea. He also constantly praised the Shurangama Mantra and the merit gained from reciting it. He especially commended the three Mahayana sutras: the Shurangama Sutra, the Dharma Flower Sutra and the Flower Adornment Sutra. Preeminent ones have said, "The Shurangama leads us to enlightenment, the Dharma Flower leads us to Buddhahood." Hence, we naturally start with the Shurangama Sutra. In Roll Seven of the Shurangama Sutra, the World Honored One continuously praised the merit of this spiritual mantra from different angles, such as:

All Buddhas from the ten directions realize the Unsurpassed, Proper and Pervasive Enlightenment. Thus Come Ones of the ten directions recite the heart of this mantra to tame all demons and externalists. All Thus Come Ones of the ten directions are embodied in the heart of this mantra and turn the great Dharma wheel throughout countries as numerous as motes of dust. Place a written copy of this mantra in a scented sack, on ourselves or in our homes, and we will not be harmed by any poison for the rest of our lives. We should know that anyone who recites and who teaches others to recite this mantra will not be burned by fire, drowned by water or hurt by major or minor poisons. As many Vajra Treasury King Bodhisattvas as 84,000 nayutas of sand grains in the Ganges River and their multitudes will attend to us day and night.

People who uphold the mantra will be able to recall what has occurred in as many eons past as the number of sand grains in 84,000 Ganges Rivers. Free of doubts and delusions, they know everything.

If we read or recite, write out, carry with us, or place the mantra in a concealed place and make offerings of all kinds of material goods to it, then we will not become born in poor, low-class or unpleasant places in eon after eon.

The mantra can enable people who broke their precepts to become pure again, enable those who have not received the precepts to have the opportunity to receive them, enable those who are not diligent to become diligent, enable those who are unwise to become wise, those who are impure to become pure, enable those who disobey the prohibitions on eating to once again adhere to the precepts related to eating naturally.

By reciting this mantra, serious offenses such as the five rebellious acts that deserve the retribution of being in the relentless hells and the four parajikas or the eight parajikas of

Bhikshus and Bhikshunis will disintegrate like sand scattered by a violent wind so that they are completely eliminated without a trace.

By reading, reciting, writing, wearing or upholding this mantra, or placing it in our homes, buildings or gardens, all major and minor offenses and obstructions from infinite eons until now, including those not yet repented of, will melt like snow met with hot water. We also thereby acquire the patience with the non-existence of people and dharmas soon.

Childless women who wish to become pregnant may recite this mantra sincerely or wear this sitatapatra mantra (the Shurangama Mantra) and thereby become capable of bearing and giving birth to children who have blessings, virtues and wisdom.

Those who wish for longevity will live a long life.

Placing a written version of this mantra at the gates facing each of the four directions, any caitya or dhvaja (such as at a Buddhist monastery or tied to a banner or flag) and then having everyone in the vicinity welcome this mantra with bows and respect, or having everyone wear it and make offerings to it or having everyone concentrate on it, or having everyone place it in their residences, all disasters (such as famine or plague, war or theft) will disappear naturally.

Gods and dragons will be happy at any place or country where this mantra is found and will be pleased with any being who possesses this mantra. As a result, the weather will accord with the seasons, harvests will be abundant, and everyone will be happy.

The merit from reciting this mantra is so supreme, how can we not make the resolve to accept and uphold it, read, recite, write and carry the Shurangama Mantra for our family and friends, country and society, for the benefit of ourselves and others?

Many fellow cultivators may feel that the Shurangama Mantra is too long and back away from learning it, which is unfortunate. We may need 20 minutes to chant this mantra through when we start out, but after becoming familiar with it and when in a clear state of mind, we may only need five minutes to recite this mantra, keeping a swift but unrushed pace. If we feel restless because of the speed, we may wish to recite it slowly and in a focused fashion, with no false thoughts and by enunciating each syllable. That should take ten minutes at the most. As our practice develops, we who recite it often even feel we cannot get enough of it.

I am laden with a tremendous amount of karmic obstructions and enjoy very little wisdom. When I was in junior high, I suffered profoundly due to my intense lust. Whenever thoughts of desire occurred, I had to use my will and various means to control it but they were less than effective. Little would I have guessed that after two months of practicing this mantra that this habit that had been with me for twenty years vanished immediately, without forcing it at all. The urge to smoke vanishes in the same way, making it unnecessary to use various means to quit smoking and struggle against the temptation to smoke. This feeling of purity is extremely refreshing and freeing. No wonder the World Honored One repeatedly urged us that if there are old habits we cannot eliminate, to the extent that it is difficult for us to uphold the Four Clear Instructions on Purity strictly (ending thoughts of desire, killing, stealing and huge lies), then we should practice and recite the magical Shurangama Mantra with a oneness of mind.

Nowadays, my favorite music in the car is the chanting of the magical Shurangama Mantra, which is on audio tape and CD distributed by the Dharma Realm Buddhist Books Distribution Society in Taipei. It is elegant and smooth. Someone who drinks it in feels calm, carefree, and refreshed. The 27th chapter of the Nirvana Sutra states, "The Samadhi of the Foremost Shurangama has five names, one is the Samadhi of the Foremost Shurangama, two is Prajna Paramita, three is Vajra Samadhi, four is the Samadhi of the Lion's Roar, and five is the Buddha Nature. Its name depends on what is done with it." So if we sincerely and concentrate on reciting the magical Shurangama Mantra, why worry we will not realize the great Shurangama Samadhi, which leads to understanding our mind, seeing our inherent nature, and realizing Buddhahood? Above all, we should not forget this mantra. We should perfect the practice of reciting the Shurangama Mantra, "the king of mantras." Let us cultivate it diligently and not waste this valuable time. It is said, "A human form is difficult to acquire, but now we have it. The Buddhadharma is difficult to encounter, but now we have found it. If we do not reach the other shore and get out of suffering in this lifetime, then in what lifetime will we do so?" Furthermore, we do not want to let the Venerable Master down, after all his eager and attentive teachings and his come-again vows of compassion.

Adversities Become Auspiciousness
with the Sincere Recitation
of the Mantra

With the help of the Shurangama Sutra and Mantra, may all beings soon perfect Bodhi and realize Buddhahood.

by Gwo Jyun Jiang

My second daughter handed me a booklet of the Shurangama Mantra with phonetics for me to follow along and read. I looked it through and set it down. I continued to read the Dharma Flower Lotus Sutra's Guanshiyin Bodhisattva's Universal Door Chapter and the Buddha Speaks of Amitabha Sutra everyday. Then once, when I was done with my assignment and was putting these sutras on the altar, I noticed that green-covered Shurangama Mantra booklet standing upright on the altar. I thought it was strange because all the other sutras were lying down flat, how come this mantra book was standing? I did not even know how to pronounce the first syllable correctly. I confirmed it by checking a dictionary and thought I might as well give it a try. Little would I have guessed that as soon as I finished reading it in the morning, I did not want any meat at breakfast. My family thought it was strange that someone who had been wishing to become a vegetarian actually officially became one on that day. It was a real miracle. I thought it was very strange too. After reciting the Shurangama Mantra in the morning, I felt fresh and did not want any meat. Although I had been wanting to become a vegetarian for a long time, I was always too gluttonous; my head was usually filled with the tastes of meat dishes. I could not even be completely vegetarian for two days out of the month. Only at breakfast was I able to gain a little control. Unexpectedly though, after practicing the Shurangama Mantra, my usual behavior changed radically and I was able to become a complete vegetarian. My husband bellowed: "Xiaofeng," he ordered my daughter, "hurry up and go buy some crispy, delicious Kentucky fried chicken, Mom's favorite. Also get some mashed potatoes topped with gravy." I was unmoved by what I heard. It was really incredible. I really could be a vegetarian! I decided to put aside other practices and concentrate on the Shurangama Mantra. At first I felt ashamed of myself for abandoning my daily recitation of the Universal Door Chapter and Amitabha Sutra. I was reluctant to let these practices go and felt guilty too. On three different occasions, I took up these practices again; but I just did not feel as pure and carefree as when I recited the mantra. Cultivation is personal. It is fine as long as it works for you. It is just as the Venerable Master said: "each practice is an antidote that the Buddhas and Bodhisattvas created to cure living beings' sickness." The Shurangama Mantra must be my medication!

I get up in the middle of the night at 2:30 a.m. and start to recite the Mantra at 3 a.m. five, seven, and up to 19 times. At first it took me an hour to go through it once, but gradually I was able to go through it once by heart in 15 minutes. I recite as if not reciting so that there are two entities: one is reciting continuously, as if apart from the original entity so that I do not really know who is reciting. Another entity though is relaxed and at ease, having nothing to do with the recitation. It is just pure and untainted. If I think about it then there is the one who recites by memory. If I do not think about it, then I become one with that which is reciting the Mantra in a state that is pure and without thoughts. After I am finished reciting it from memory, I feel pure and happy. I respond to things as they come and let go as things go. I do not think about the past, present or future, clearing away these thoughts so that I face, accept, and deal with things as they come. Once things pass, then calm is restored like a boat crossing over an ocean. When the boat comes, waves rage but when the boat passes, the waves die down and the water becomes calm. After practicing this mantra for a long time, the turbulent waves raged no more, they remain unaffected, as if an individual entity not turned by any external phenomenon. After a longer period of time, one can control external states like watching television. One can change the channel immediately when the content is no good. One can turn to channel two when channel three is no good. Like a battery-operated remote control, one will automatically switch channels without thinking. All external phenomena change channels as if automatically controlled by remote. We still need to use our fingers to press the remote to control a television, an electronic toy, or a remote car, but given mantra practice, we can change the state we face automatically and at will. When we first start to learn we still have to change the state by thinking; after a while, it becomes natural and external states and us become isolated entities. Each is a distinct entity that does not obstruct the other; they go their own ways. The mind is pure and becomes a distinct entity free of thoughts and defilement, unaffected and as it is. External phenomena cannot enter. There is no you or me. Although we hear sounds of criticism, the subject of the criticism no longer exists. (Before I practiced the mantra, I could be deeply hurt when criticized. It was worse than being stabbed. After reciting the Mantra, "you" and "I" no longer exist, so the subject of the criticism exists no longer.) Arrows cannot enter either. When external states shoot arrows at us, a protective membrane deflects them so they drop to one side. One remains as one is and unaffected, as if one possessed a Vajra indestructible body. External states include people, phenomena, with the underlying noumena. They can no longer affect and shake "the mind that is just as it is and unaffected." Instead it can change channels automatically. How supreme!

When I returned to Taiwan in 1994, I received a complimentary copy of the Shurangama Sutra. I was taken aback to read in the Sutra that those who cannot keep to the prohibitions of being a vegetarian will be able to do so if they recite the mantra. No wonder I became a total vegetarian after reading the Shurangama Mantra. The Shurangama Sutra explains all this. It really works! This is why I further believe in every word and every line in the Buddhist sutras. The Shurangama Mantra is the heart of the Buddhas' mantras, and so it is easy to succeed with it. 1) The Dharma of Achievement — being pure in the three karmas of body, mouth and mind. 2) The Dharma of Benefits — upholding the mantra can enhance one's spiritual practice. 3) The Dharma that Shatters Evil — upholding the mantra can break all bad habits. 4) The Dharma that Quell Disasters — eliminating all disasters. 5) The Dharma of Hooking and Summoning — being able to capture demons and ghosts no matter how far away they are. 6) The Dharma that Subdues — taming and subduing all monsters, demons and evil spells. 7) The Auspicious Dharma — upholding this Mantra sincerely, everything will go as we wish, adversities will turn into auspiciousness and hundreds of other beneficial things will happen. If we can practice this mantra with the compassionate wish to save beings, then we will definitely eliminate disasters and realize Unsurpassed, Proper, Equal and Right Enlightenment in the future.

The Shurangama Sutra describes the power of wearing the Shurangama Mantra. It is divided into five divisions, which represent its powers. 1) The Eastern Vajra Division – The five Vajra mantras with Akshobhya Buddha as the host of this division. 2) The Southern Jeweled Division – The five mantras of all gods. The Jeweled Production Buddha is the host of this division. 3) The Central Buddha Division – all mantras of Buddhas. Vairochana Buddha is the host of this division. 4) The Western Lotus Division – all mantras of Bodhisattvas. Amitabha Buddha is the host of this division. 5) The Northern Karma Division – all mantras of ghosts and spirits. Accomplishment Buddha is the host of this division. Because there are five major demon armies in this world, there are Buddhas in five areas here to suppress them. By wearing or writing out this mantra or placing it on the walls of our homes, we will enjoy a life of never being harmed by any poisons. If we read and recite it respectfully, write it out

respectfully or wear it or make offerings to it at our place of residency, then past karma we accumulated in many eons will melt instantaneously, as if snow met with boiling water. Since past obstructions have been eliminated, the proper samadi will come forth. We will soon realize the patience with the non-existence of people and dharmas. If one had committed major offenses worthy of being in the relentless hells, such as the five rebellious acts, then based on the power of this mantra, all major offenses will disappear completely, leaving not a trace, just like a fierce wind blowing away a cluster of sand. Furthermore, no demons or ghosts, none of our enemies since beginningless time, no accidents, past karma, disasters or past debtors will come and disturb us or hurt us. Any mantra, spell, black magic, poison, metallurgical poisons, toxic vapors from any grass, tree, insect, snake or other things will turn into the best-tasting sweet dew in the mouth of someone who practices this mantra. Not to mention the pesticides on vegetables in Taiwan or other viruses. One is immune to them. After I began to practice this mantra, I became healthier and flues stayed far away from me so that I am relaxed and carefree.

Due to the length of this piece, I will not write out each benefit. To learn about them in detail, read the Shurangama Sutra to get a glimpse of how wonderful they are. You will enjoy it as you would drinking sweet dew or the finest cream.

When I learned about this wonderful king of mantras, I immediately wrote out this mantra at dawn and hung it on the fence of our garden and home to ensure our safety. Furthermore, everyone in the family wore it and benefited a lot from it. For example, when our electricity at home went out, I went to check on the meter and my husband hid in some dark place—it was a trick of his to hide in order to try to scare me. But I no longer reacted with fear. I was not at all afraid. I was very calm. My heart does not beat thunderously when I hear a sudden scream or a strange sound. My heart does not palpitate. My "mind" is always very quiet, stable and balanced. This happens naturally without forcing it at all. Conversely, I recall that before I began practicing the mantra, the situation was the exact opposite. My heart would beat like crazy and my whole being would be ill at ease due to shock. I would experience spasms and the like. I was completely different before and after. We can tell then that we do not necessarily have to meditate to reach Samadhi. The Thus Come One's Samadhi is Samadhi while walking, standing, sitting and lying down. The Foremost Shurangama's great and profound Samadhi is so supreme! Samadhi gives rise to wisdom. We have heard that the Shurangama enlightens and the Dharma Flower enables us to realize Buddhahood. To realize Buddhahood, we must first plant seeds for Buddhahood, which means to accept the practice of the Shurangma Sutra and/or Mantra first. We will reap the fruit of the seeds that we sow. If we plant seeds for Buddhahood, we will bear the fruit of Buddhahood. If we plant the causes for being Bodhisattvas, we will bear the fruits for being Bodhisattvas. Although every being has the Buddha nature and will eventually realize Buddhahood by listening to the sutras, hearing the Dharma and studying Buddhism, one must go through the four stages of "believing, understanding, practicing and realizing". For example, by accepting and practicing the Shurangama Sutra and/or Mantra, we have already planted the causes for Buddhahood. We must continue to work hard so that we are diligent with our mind and body, day and night; so that we uphold the precepts and end greed, hatred and delusion; so that we cultivate the non-outflow studies of precepts, Samadhi and wisdom, and hence perfect Bodhi and reap the fruit of Buddhahood for certain.

The day of my father's funeral, I hand-wrote a copy of the Shurangama Mantra for my family members to wear. The Taipei No. 1 Mortuary also gave everyone a spell drawn on a red piece of paper. My youngest sister was in a hurry and did not find the bag with several copies of the hand-written mantra in it so she wore the spell that the mortuary gave. Who would have known that after she left the crematorium she could not get out of bed the next morning? All the bones in her body ached, her head ached, her back ached. She thought she would get better if she slept a bit more but she became worse the day after. I was on the alert and wondered if it was that spell. I gave the Shurangama Mantra that I had on me to her to wear. She immediately recovered and got out of bed. It was really incredible. Later I found a smaller and more exquisitely made Shurangama Mantra in the shops and thought it should be exchanged for the several heavy and inconvenient pieces of hand-written paper. It would be much lighter. She resisted and refused to make the change. She was only willing to make the exchange when I told her that the content is the same. This is how much she believed in what she had.

My oldest daughter and friends came to South Africa to visit during March of 1996 and traveled to more than a few famous scenic spots and ancient sites. She woke me up in the middle of the night after a day of travel, and told me that she was dreaming about a lot of scary things. She was terrified and could not sleep. I wondered why she was not wearing the Shurangama Mantra around her neck. I had given away the Shurangama Mantras I had on hand to two friends who had car accidents before. In a panic, I rose and searched until I found one for her to wear so she could go back to her room and sleep. She slept until morning and did not come looking for me, so I did not worry any more.

In October of 1997, my youngest daughter was at a church near her school and saw a deceased white man. She was feeling dizzy and sleepy when she got home. She was feeling somewhat strange. She did not wear the Shurangama Mantra. She said that her school forbid students to wear necklaces and other decorative items. Though I had pinned the Shurangama Mantra to the inside of her collar before, she had changed her uniform and forgot to re-pin it. Once she put it on, she felt a coolness coming down from her head and felt more comfortable. Now she never forgets to wear it.

My oldest son passed away in July of 1995. When he was

seriously ill, I had him wear a hand-written Shurangama Mantra. When my oldest son was three months old, he had an extremely high fever and became seriously retarded. Normally, I did not bother him when he did not want to wear the mantra, but when he was seriously ill, I forced it on him. The Shurangama Sutra says, "If one reads, recites, writes, wears, stores it or make offerings to the mantra, using all kinds of material items, one will not become born in impoverished, lowly or unpleasant places." My son passed away in July of 1995. I believe that the power of greatly kind and compassionate Amitabha took him to the Land of Ultimate Bliss. Some nine hours after he passed away, his whole body was cold except for the top of his head. His forehead, though only an inch down was as cold as ice. He was close by but we were worlds apart. He had a smile and a pleasant look on his face as he left.

By practicing the Shurangama Sutra and Mantra, one will naturally radiate a light of wisdom while in the great Samadhi. One will not be selfish, pursue self-interests, be greedy, keep seeking, be contentious or dishonest. When one's mind is scattered and one is about to speak casually, one will naturally pull in one's thoughts and cultivate so that one's mind is not disturbed but will naturally gain Samadhi. When one wants to throw a temper tantrum, one will remain "patient" and with a tender heart and voice, make the other party happy. Consequently, "patience" disappears completely, vanishing in the thin air. Wherefore had "patience" come? One is just happy everyday.

I hope everyone will practice the teachings that plant the seeds for Buddhahood—the Shurangama Sutra and Mantra. May all beings soon perfect Bodhi and realize the fruit of Buddhahood.

I now dedicate my life to the
Great Buddha at the Crown

And to the illuminating wisdom in
the infinite Dharma Treasury.

I vow to gain clear understanding
of this wondrous Dharani,

And reverently practice according to
the intent of the Thus Come Ones.

Recite the Shurangama Mantra
to Save the World

The Venerable Master said that when the world nears its end, if one person can single-mindedly recite the Shurangama Mantra, the world can be saved.

by Ryh-Syang Lin

In 1990, my aunt took my family to visit Gold Wheel Monastery in Los Angeles. I was 10 when I first encountered the concepts of Buddhism. I remember my parents yearning for spiritual guidance when their restaurant went out of business. I think they found what they where looking for. A year later, my parents sent my sister, my brother, and myself up to the City of Ten Thousand Buddhas to study at Instilling Goodness and Developing Virtue Schools (IGDVS). On my first trip up to the City of Ten Thousand Buddhas, I was amazed by the ten thousand statues of the Buddhas and told my mom that I would like to be that Buddha, pointing to a statue on the wall. I asked her, "Do I have to leave the home life to become a Buddha?" She told me that it would be a faster path to become a Buddha. I did not understand much about Buddhism at the time.

I learned more about Buddhism in my Buddhist Studies classes at IGDVS. I also attended ceremonies in the Buddha Hall and my parents instilled Buddhist values and traditions in me. When I was thirteen years old, my mother wanted me to memorize the Shurangama Mantra after listening to the Venerable Abbot's [Master Hua's] lecture on the benefits of the Shurangama Mantra. The length of the Mantra overwhelmed me and I did not think it would be possible to memorize. However, my mom's Dharma friend, Mrs. Wong from Gold Wheel Monastery, convinced me to do so. With her encouragement, I started memorizing two lines a day. As I was memorizing the Mantra, I felt very safe and grew more interested in it, because the Venerable Master said that when the world nears its end, if one person can single-mindedly recite the Shurangama Mantra, the world can be saved. My quota for memorizing increased from two lines per day to 5, 10, and 20 lines per day, until I finished the Mantra two months later. My mom told me to recite it every day so that I did not forget it. I ended up reciting it once before going to school, once after school, and once before bedtime, on my own initiative. In retrospect, I believe I was compelled by the great cause of keeping the Shurangama in the world and saving the world.

This cause led me to want to uphold the Five Precepts. I had been observing the precepts for two years already and I proposed this idea to my mom. [Editor's note: Upasaka Lin took refuge at CTTB on July 13, 1991, with his sister and brother. He was a seventh grader in 1993 and received the Five Precepts when he was almost thirteen years old.] She was really surprised and wanted reassurance that I would not kill or harm life, steal, engage in sexual misconduct, take any intoxicants, or lie to the end of my life. I told her that I would not do those things. I took the Five Precepts on Guanyin Bodhisattva's Birthday with my good friend Peter Gan. These precepts became my criteria for all my decisions in life. I was really put to the test after graduating from Developing Virtue Secondary School in 1997. The outside world was difficult to adjust to. I was often tempted to do things that were in direct violation to the precepts. Being aware of the precepts, I refrained from violating them.

I had many struggles with my parents during my college years. I shared similar experiences with other kids who grew up on Buddhist principles instilled by our parents. I had a bad temper that prevailed during my childhood. I always tried to control and suppress my anger, but in the end my anger was still present. After a stressful semester in my senior year at Berkeley, I attended the Dharma Realm Buddhist Youth Shurangama Winter Retreat in 2000, so that I could get away from city life. I became more aware of my state of mind and the attachments to my preconceived notions of "objects" and "people" which were the direct cause of my frustration, dissatisfaction, and suffering.

After getting some insights, I wanted to work on my bad habits and improve them. I started with small things that were directly related to my anger, such as being aware of my anger on the road when driving to and from school. I was a dangerous driver when I was angry. I became aware each time and observed the heat of my anger rising and how it was about to explode. I was told by Dharma Master Heng Sure that a Zen Master in the U.S. said, "Leave the front and back doors of your mind open. Let the guests come but do not serve them tea." With this understanding, I realized that the people who cut me off on the streets are the guests and my anger exploding was the result of serving the guests tea. Bit by bit, I just let go of my attachments to these thoughts. As a result, these thoughts passed through but were not served tea.

I tried to apply this to all aspects of my shortcomings. It was not an easy thing to do; in fact it was very difficult. Because I recognized that these attachments to thoughts were the direct cause of my frustration and suffering, I wanted to change them. This gave me the perseverance to try to be a better person. People who want to change and become better are practicing the Buddhadharma, no matter what their faith or religion is. We can only change ourselves and not others. When people see a change in you, they too will awaken by noticing the difference in you.

If You Sincerely Wish to Be Good, Do Not Be Afraid when Demons Come to Test You

From then on, he always slept with the Shurangama Mantra on him whenever he went out. For six years, he has slept peacefully without any disturbance.

by Teow Chuan Lim
compiled by Fuali Hsieh

Upasaka Lim Teow Chuan (Dharma name: Guo Chuan), is a retired official of the Malaysian government. This year (1998) he led eleven fellow cultivators to the City of Ten Thousand Buddhas to attend the Jeweled Repentance before the Ten Thousand Buddhas. Having made such a long journey, participating in the session full-time was a test of their stamina, especially considering the great variation in temperature between morning and evening at the City of Ten Thousand Buddhas. At the end of the Dharma session, I, Upasaka Lim was all smiles. Clearly, he was filled with faith and Dharma bliss during this Dharma banquet.

Special circumstances led Upasaka Lim to take refuge with the Venerable Master. In 1988, while leading his disciples on a Dharma tour in Asia, the Master was preparing to go from Taiwan to Malaysia, but had not yet obtained a visa. At that critical moment, a lawyer friend asked Upasaka Lim to help, since he had worked in the immigration agency before and was the then chief secretary of the vice-president of the Youth Culture and Physical Education Department. Although Upasaka Lim was not yet the Master's disciple, he sent documents and met with immigration officials; consequently the visa was granted within a week's time.

"Really, I should have taken refuge with the Venerable Master then. It is too bad I did not recognize what kind of a man was in front of me, and only took refuge four years later (1992)." He had already met and talked with the Master, yet he missed his opportunity. Upasaka Lim recounted this incident with a sigh. However, he believes that he did plant good roots then; the time just was not ripe yet. "To be frank, I was not that interested in Buddhism then. I was just doing a favor for a friend, nothing more."

It so happened that when Dharma Master Heng Sure led a delegation to Malaysia in 1992, the group also had problems going through customs. By then Upasaka Lim was working in the Malaysian Printing Bureau. The organizing committee for the delegation, a new group whose members did not know Upasaka Lim, suddenly showed up at his door and asked for his help again; and the delegation obtained visas without problem.

Upasaka Lim could not figure it out: Why was it that both times when the Master or his disciples came to Malaysia and had difficulty at customs, he was called upon? He did not even know the organizers of the visit, and he himself had already changed jobs. He concluded that perhaps there were past affinities which he could not escape, so he had better return to the ranks, take refuge with the Triple Jewel, and become the Master's disciple.

"If you want to be good, karmic obstacles will seek you out. If you want to become a Buddha, you must first endure the demons." A few days after he took refuge, the demons showed up. One night when he went out to get gas, an elderly woman refused to get out of his way and asked for a ride. Finally he let her get into the car.

As soon as she entered the car, Upasaka Lim smelled a foul odor and could hardly breathe. She also started to make a lot of vulgar gestures and said suggestively, "Do not worry, I have no husband." Her words gave Upasaka Lim goose bumps. He was sure that she was a demon. He started to shiver in fear. He had only recently taken refuge, and had not even learned to recite any mantras to help him out.

Fortunately he had a flash of inspiration and started to recite "Namo Amitabha Buddha" without thinking. As soon as he recited, the foul smell disappeared and the woman stopped flirting. But when he stopped reciting, she began moving her hands and feet again, and so he immediately resumed the recitation. After battling like this for five minutes, she finally got out of the car, saying to him, "You are a good person, and your life will be good." She then got out and he never saw her again.

From that evening forward, Upasaka Lim often mumbled in his sleep. His wife, who had taken refuge with the Venerable Master in 1988, begged the Master to save him. When a disciple was in trouble, how could the teacher stand by and watch? The Master asked Upasaka Lim to come to the City of Ten Thousand Buddhas. The demon came to the City with him, and was outside his window for thirteen nights in a row; it seemed as if he was trying to break the door down with a hammer. Upasaka Lim was so fraught with anxiety that he only slept one hour each night—from 2:30 to 3:30 a.m., before he rushed out of bed for morning recitation.

On the 14th day, the Venerable Master came to the Buddha Hall and tapped Upasaka Lim on the head three times with his cane, saying to him, "You're fine now, you can go home." From that time on, there were no more problems. Strange, isn't it?

All these trials and tribulations inspired Upasaka Lim's interest in the Buddhadharma and faith in the Venerable Master. He knew that he had found a great and wise teacher. He became increasingly vigorous in cultivation, studied and practiced in accord with the Master's instructional talks and the Buddhist Sutras, and received the five precepts in 1997.

The Venerable Master had said that ghosts, demons, and monstrous beings are particularly numerous in Southeast Asia. As a government official, Upasaka Lim was often sent to the countryside. Sometimes at midnight he would be driving where few people had ever gone, and some strange things would happen. He had been caught in sudden downpours that only hit the front of his car; no rain fell on the other side, but he could not see through the front windshield. In such situations, he would switch on the tape of the Shurangama Mantra, and after a few minutes the rain would stop and he would be able to see the road clearly again.

One time when he was staying at a rural inn, he forgot to wear the miniature copy of the Shurangama Mantra. In the middle of the night, a ghost came to bully him. It proceeded to press down on Upasaka Lim's body and immobilizing him. It was as if his hands and feet were tied up, and he could not even open his mouth to shout for help. He felt extremely uncomfortable, as if his guts were about to burst. This was the kumbhanda ghost (winter melon ghost) described in the Shurangama Sutra. It has no hands or feet, and its body is shaped like a barrel or winter melon.

Upasaka Lim struggled for a long time before the ghost finally let him go. He immediately got out of bed, took the Shurangama Mantra booklet, and put it in his pajama pocket. Then he feigned sleep and waited eagerly to see what would happen when the ghost returned. Before he fell asleep, the ghost did return to attack him. It pressed the Upasaka's body lightly, also pressing the mantra, and was at once thrown up into the air as if it had hit a landmine. Upasaka Lim was wide awake, for he had been waiting to watch this Dharma-contest.

From then on, Upasaka Lim always slept with the Shurangama Mantra on him whenever he went out. For six years, he has slept peacefully without any disturbance.

Upasaka Lim has also used the Great Compassion Mantra and water over which the Mantra has been recited to save his dying pet dog. Two years ago, he mistakenly used kerosene to bathe the little dog, hoping to get rid of its lice. After the dog had been soaked in kerosene for a little while, it could no longer stand up. The dog shut its eyes and was barely breathing. The vet examined the dog and said that the kerosene had penetrated the skin through some wounds and had already entered the bloodstream, poisoning the blood. He said the dog would die within three hours and

there was nothing he
could do.

Upasaka Lim had no
choice but to bring the dog
home. His family prayed to
Guanyin Bodhisattva to help
the dog. By that time, foam
was coming out of its mouth,
and it could not move, eat,
or drink. His family recited the
Great Compassion Mantra 108 times
over water, and then placed the water drop by drop into the
dog's closed mouth. They also made a vow on behalf of the
dog, saying that if it lived, it would be vegetarian for the rest
of its life.

On the third day, a miracle happened. A breeze blew over
the unconscious dog, and it suddenly started vomiting. Then
it got up on its feet. A week later it was fully recovered. The
week after that, it completely shed all of its fur and turned
into an ugly, bald little dog. A few weeks after that, it grew
new fur. The dog began to eat vegetarian food and often sat
at the door listening to the family recite Sutras and do the
morning and evening recitations, as if it also wished to be
reborn in the Land of Ultimate Bliss.

The great mantra of great compassion penetrates
    heaven and earth.
One hundred recitations for one thousand days
    cause ten kings to rejoice.
Its great compassion and kindness cure all disease;
And so an announcement is projected high upon
    the offense screen.

This verse composed by the Venerable Master describes the miraculous functioning of the Great Compassion Mantra. If one recites it 108 times every day, the ten King Yamas will utter joyful praise. Curing illness, prolonging life, and reviving the dead are some of its small functions. Liberating one from birth and death and bringing one to Buddhahood are the great functions of the Great Compassion Mantra.

She Recited the Shurangama Mantra
Seeking to Become A Nun—

At that time, all I could think of was come to the City of Ten Thousand Buddhas. So I recited and bowed the Shurangama Mantra everyday.

by Bhikshuni Heng Shen

I lived with my grand-mother for a while when I was eleven years old. She was a Buddhist who had taken refuge with the Triple Jewel. Whenever there was a retreat or a session, grandma would take me to the temple. My recollections of the monastics were very vague, but the vegetarian food made quite an impression on me. It was so much better than meat dishes. Therefore, even though the walk was much more than an hour, I did not feel tired. Someone told me to chant "Na Mo A Mi Do Po Ye..." (Rebirth Mantra) because this mantra could make me smarter. Being devoted, I recited it often. I continued reciting this mantra even after I left grandma's home and stopped visiting temples with her. When I rediscovered Buddhism later on, I realized that it was the Rebirth Mantra I had been reciting all along.

I worked at a vegetarian restaurant in Taiwan in 1989. A colleague there gave me two books by the Venerable Master: Commentary on the Earth Store Sutra and Dharma Talks by Venerable Master Hua, Volume One. I read them in no time and was inspired to profound faith. I could not wait, so I went to Dharma Realm Buddhist Books Distribution Society in Taipei and requested two more books.

At that time, all I could think of was to come to the City of Ten Thousand Buddhas (CTTB). One day, I dreamed that I was doing one bow every three steps to CTTB. The Venerable Master walked up in front of me and rubbed my head and said, "You can come to CTTB." At that very moment, my entire body felt cleansed and refreshed. I woke up with great joy and vividly remembered that cleansing state.

My wish to leave the home-life conflicted with my responsibility of being a filial daughter until my father passed away. I made a vow to Guanyin Bodhisattva that I would leave the home-life within three years. My wish came true. I finally arrived at CTTB and became a nun on March 25, 1995. In 2000, I received the complete ordination Precepts.

Our Genuine Home is Right Here

Every morning I get up early and bow to the Shurangama Mantra. I make a prostration to each line.

by Gwo Zhao Pan

I love to read the Venerable Master Hsuan Hua's Instructional Talks, because everything he says has great significance. After reading his instructions, I realized that life is short and that I should not waste my life by not cultivating. Every morning I get up early and bow to the Shurangama Mantra. I make a prostration to each line. I feel it is essential to bow. If I do not work hard, my inherent wisdom will not come forth. If we wish to bring forth our inherent wisdom, then we must apply effort. I sit in meditation at night. In the beginning, folding my legs was so painful, but I told myself to bear the pain because one must endure a little suffering in studying Buddhism.

I have cataracts. When I sit in meditation, my eyelids do not close. Since my eyes have to stay open, the light keeps me from being able to contemplate. I went to Guanyin Bodhisattva and said, "This disciple has an eye problem. My eyelids cannot close and I have not been able to meditate." Who would have guessed that after I said that, the minute I sat down, a light shone upon me and my eyelids naturally closed? Rays of light radiated upon me once again, and when I opened my eyes, I saw that they came from Guanyin Bodhisattva. The Bodhisattva was bestowing his compassionate blessings! Gradually my eyes improved, and now they are completely well.

I get up at six o'clock every morning. After I drink some water, I start to bow to Amitabha Buddha. Then I bow for half an hour to the Shurangama Mantra. Following that, I sit in meditation for the duration of two incense sticks, until ten in the morning. Afterwards, I do full prostrations with my entire body down to the ground. From that practice, every disease of mine such as arthritis has gone away. It is incredible! I was so ignorant, for I studied sutras without understanding them. Now when I read sutras with a calm mind, I understand them naturally. During the Ten Thousand Buddhas Repentance at the City of Ten Thousand Buddhas, every time I bowed down, the next Buddha's name would pop up in my mind. I did not understand why this amazing thing happened. If we are sincere, we will certainly experience responses.

I do not think of anything else except that I am good for nothing and must cultivate quickly. Coming to a monastery is like coming home. We are old and must quickly recite the Buddha's name. Gold Buddha Monastery is our genuine home. We must cultivate hard, or else we will end up being left out all the time. We must diligently bow and cultivate so as to penetrate the truth. When we study Buddhism with sincerity, we will have responses. I have so many responses from Guanyin Bodhisattva to talk about. Next time I will say more.

Fellow cultivators! Everything the Venerable Master Hua said is absolutely true! He taught us that cultivation means not to have false thoughts. I used to wonder how false thoughts could be smashed. I realize now that if we honestly cultivate everyday, false thoughts will cease. The afflictions accumulated from our past cover us like a hat. We can take off that hat of afflictions that weighs down upon our heads. My daughter's terminal breast cancer did not bother me. Old or young, we will all go. It does not matter if we depart earlier. All of us should apply more effort in studying Buddhism. We should not wander outside; our genuine home is right here!

Shurangama Mantra:
How profound its merit!

> As long as we are willing to cultivate according to the Dharma and Vinya, we will naturally turn calamities into blessings.
>
> by Bhikshuni Heng Mao

August 20th, 2002 was a unusual day that became unusual because six people at the City of the Dharma Realm (CDR) were poisoned simultaneously. Ambulances took the poisoned victims to varying degrees to the emergency rooms of three nearby hospitals.

It was my turn to work in the office the morning of the incident. I took my food to the office at 11 a.m. When I took that first bite of boiled vegetables, I thought it was extremely bitter but I did not mind it. But it was still extremely bitter on the second bite. I thought I should learn to take what is bitter. It was not until my third or fourth bite that I felt things were not right. It was way too bitter. My lips began to go numb and a thought flashed in my head: "There is something wrong with these vegetables!" I went to the dining hall immediately and told everyone not to eat any more.

When I stepped into the dining hall, Heng Chan Shi was coming my way and told me that there was something wrong with the vegetables. I rushed to tell everyone not to eat any more of this vegetable. At the same time I went into the kitchen to ask for water with brown sugar. Everyone should be given a glass to detoxify their systems, I instructed. Later, I walked back to the office and halfway there I heard someone ringing the bell at the front gate. I opened the gate, but then I completely lost consciousness. I do not remember how I got sent to the hospital.

Below is what I learned when we later had a meeting reflecting on this event. People found me in my room. I was sitting by the restroom door and staring blankly. I did not react no matter how they pushed or yelled at me. Several people carried me onto the ambulance. During the ride, the medical staff saw that my pupils were turned up and that I was foaming at the mouth, so they rushed to save me with an oxygen mask. When I went into the emergency room, six large men pressed me down to do emergency enemas and intestinal examinations. The doctor also said that I needed to stay in the hospital and be under observation for two to three days.

At eight-thirty that night, Ms. Chen, a laywoman at CDR, came to the hospital to see me and asked me if I was doing better. I was not quite conscious yet, so I heard what she said to me, but I only saw strings of words in my head, the meaning of which I could not grasp. This lasted until the next morning when Cathi (now the novice nun Jin Huan Shi) was by my side and taking care of me. I asked her what time it was and she said, "Almost four in the morning." "Oh, then I have to get up to do morning ceremony." I rushed to find my sash. When I got my sash on, I was doing the morning ceremony on the sickbed. When that was finished at 5 a.m. and according to the CDR schedule, it was time to recite the Shurangama Mantra. It was not until I recited the Shurangama Mantra three times, as we typically do at CDR, that I woke up completely. I realized then that I was in the hospital and was sent there because I had been poisoned.

All of a sudden I thought of a passage in the Shurangama Sutra that talked about the benefits of reciting the Shurangama Mantra: During the time when the Dharma is on its decline, living beings who recite or teach others to recite this mantra will not be burned by fire, drowned by flood, or harmed by major or minor poisons. Furthermore, no evil mantras of dragons, gods, ghosts and spirits, goblins, earth gods, demons and ogres can touch them. They will maintain proper feelings. All spells and curses, hateful black magic, poisonous medication, toxins from gold and silver, venomous vapors from grass, trees, insects, snakes and all things will taste like sweet dew in the mouths of these individuals.

I know the Shurangama Mantra has the power to dissolve poison. I also thought of how last night Cathi kept telling me to drink more water and go to the restroom. I sat up and crossed my legs and began to recite the Shurangama Mantra. Starting from 5 a.m. until 7:30 a.m., I recited and drank water. I drank several large glassesful of water. I started wanting to go to the restroom. I ran back and forth several times. My stool was a dark black and my urine was red.

By eight, I felt that I had recovered by about 80 to 90 percent. In addition, I thought about how expensive the medical fees were, so I wanted to ask the doctors if I might leave the hospital. When the doctor came in, I was smiling and looking quite energetic. The doctor saw this and agreed to release me from the hospital.

It was nearly meal-offering time when we drove back to CDR. Since other fellow cultivators who had been poisoned were still in the hospital, everyone was busy, so I even came back in time to help be the cantor for the meal offering!

After this incident, several things touched me deeply. I wish to share them below:

(1) The power of everyone cultivating together in a monastery is amazing. The daily morning and evening ceremonies and other ceremonies in the Buddha Hall after some time become a part of our biological clock. We will be ready to do it whenever it is that time. Even when we are unconscious, we will do them subconsciously. Naturally, we will save ourselves during critical moments between life and death.

(2) I profoundly realize the merit and wonderful use of the Shurangama Mantra. The Buddha was indeed someone "who spoke the truth and did what he said." Not only is the principle of the Shurangama Sutra this way, every Dharma the Buddha taught is true. As long as we are willing to cultivate according to the Dharma and the Vinaya, we will naturally turn calamities into blessings, turn disasters into auspicious events, and develop our Bodhi.

(3) Out of those poisoned this time, there were some who saw the ghost of impermanence. We had escaped the claws of death and felt the impermanence of life with this incident. The Saha World is not a place where we should yearn to stay. Think, we were in a monastery, a place where we thought to be the safest. We were eating vegetables we planted ourselves, which we thought to be the most reliable (note: the poisonous wild vegetable we had was jimsonweed. It looks very much like the vegetables that we typically plant

so they were accidentally picked and eaten).

Despite all that, we faced such serious threat to our lives. In short, we should hurry up and honestly collect the resources we need for heading to rebirth. Seeking to become reborn in the Land of the Ultimate Bliss is the most ultimate.

Learning to Recite the Shurangama Mantra!

Before actually starting to learn to recite the Shurangama Mantra, it is important to build a foundation in proper knowledge and views to set the path for further cultivation.

by Rich Sloger

In the Shurangama Sutra Volume One, the Venerable Master Hsuan Hua recalls the Great Tian Tai Master Zhi Ze's aspirations to encounter the Shurangama Sutra. "When the Great Master Zhi Ze heard of the existence of the Shurangama Sutra, which he had never seen, he was moved to bow to the west in hope that he would one day be able to see this Sutra. He bowed to the west every day for eighteen years, but in the end he never had the opportunity to see the Sutra." So, we, who have had the opportunity to encounter it, should not take it lightly, but should utilize every opportunity to study the Shurangama Sutra and recite the Shurangama Manta.

Studying the Shurangama Sutra and reciting the Shurangama Mantra are essential steps to take in the process of cultivation. Ultimately, the goal from this study and recitation is to end the outflows of the six sense organs (eyes, ears, nose, tongue, body, and mind) and to see our original face and obtain Shurangama Samadhi. The collection of talks by the Venerable Master Hsuan Hua entitled "A Sure Sign of the Proper Dharma" describes many of the inconceivable aspects and methods of cultivation regarding this Sutra and Mantra. I hope that sharing my experiences learning the Shurangama Mantra will help others to study and recite the Shurangama Sutra and the Shurangama Mantra.

In the Shurangama Sutra Volume One, the Venerable Master uses the verses by the Great Master Shen Hsiu and the Great Master the Sixth Patriarch to emphasis the need to cultivate both the provisional Dharma to purify the mind and to cultivate the enlightened, eternally-durable Dharma to realize the ultimate inherent wisdom.

"Great Master Shen Hsiu's verse says:

> The body is a Bodhi tree;
> The mind is like a bright mirror stand.
> Time and again brush it clean;
> Let no dust alight.

He is telling us to constantly cultivate, to time and again brush clean the mind so that it does not catch any dust.

The Great Master, the Sixth Patriarch, said in reply:

> Originally Bodhi has no tree,
> Nor any mirror stand bright.
> Originally there is not one thing,
> Where can the dust alight?

When not one thought is produced, the Buddha-nature and Samadhi appear. When your eyes, ears, nose, tongue, body, and mind suddenly move and take control, it is as if the sky has suddenly clouded over.

So in cultivation we should constantly "brush clean the mind" while also expanding our inherent, fundamental wisdom. While doing good deeds and practicing proper conduct are external methods that help clean up the mind, other practices like reciting the Shurangama Mantra and studying the Shurangama Sutra are more subtly methods to help us identify with and expand our fundamental wisdom. Methods for cultivating this fundamental wisdom are also included in many other practices. For example, a verse in the Great Compassion Repentance ceremony states that, "Above it is all Buddhas; below it is equal to all living things…". Also, the Heart Sutra states, "…All Dharmas are empty of characteristics… Therefore in emptiness there is no form, feeling, cognition, formation, or consciousness; no eyes, ears, nose, tongue, body, or mind…". And, when taking refuge with the Triple Jewel, the repentance verse ends with wish to "return to the fundamental source of the mind which is ultimately pure." All these methods of cultivation are pointing us along with the Shurangama Sutra and Shurangama Mantra to cultivate our true, inherent nature Shurangama Samadhi.

My first step toward learning to recite the Shurangama Mantra was to develop a purpose for reciting this Mantra. Although I heard the Shurangama Mantra recited by others many times and was even encouraged to learn it, I did not understand much of its importance or feel a need to study it until I read about this Mantra in the Venerable Master's collection of talks in the book A Sure Sign of the Proper Dharma. It says:

"Therefore, in Buddhism it is said that if there is even one person in the world who can recite the Shurangama Mantra, then the demons, goblins, and all the other weird creatures will not dare to openly show themselves in the world. If not even one person can recite the Shurangama Mantra from memory, then at that point all the demons, goblins, ghosts, and all the other weird creatures will appear in the world. They will wreak havoc, but no one will recognize them."

Before actually starting to learn to recite the Shurangama Mantra, it is important to build a foundation in proper knowledge and views to set the path for further cultivation. My first steps were to take refuge with the Triple Jewel and take the 5 lay people precepts. Also, I was advised to first learn to recite the Great Compassion Mantra, Ten Small Mantras, and Heart Sutra before starting to learn the Shurangama Manta.

When I first went to the monastery to follow along in the recitation book while the Dharma Masters recited the Shurangama Mantra, it was very difficult, seemingly impossible to just keep my place in the book. Before the recitation, I looked through the recitation book setting a path through the Mantra text to follow. However, as soon as the recitation began I quickly lost my place and got disoriented, to the point of not even knowing what page the recitation was on. After attending several more recitations at the monastery, following along became easier and eventually I became to recognize certain sounds that where repeated. So not knowing any more, I would look for those sections and just wait for the recitation to reach that point and then skip ahead to the next set of sounds that I recognized. Eventually, more and more sounds became recognizable and the five sections became distinct. Then, it was possible to follow along in the book during the complete recitation.

At the same time, I also listened to the tape of the Mantra at home and would try to write out the sounds to aid in memorizing them. This started with the first sound and progressed sound by sound. As I learned one sound I would go back and repeat all the other sounds up to that point. This helped to establish a recitation rhythm and reinforce the sounds that were already learned.

However after a while of practicing this way, I began to get discouraged. It seemed to be progressing too slowly and I began to feel pressure from myself that I was not doing well enough. It was taking too long. I did not think that I would ever be able to complete learning the entire Mantra. I did not want to give up, but I really was not sure what to do. Then, it occurred to me that reciting the Shurangama Mantra every day was the important thing. It really did not matter how much I could recite from memory. I would just recite the Mantra every day doing as best as I could and transfer the merit to protect all sentient beings in the Dharma Ending Age. Then, it no longer mattered how quickly I learned. In either case, I would be doing the same recitation every day whether by memory or by reading along with the tape. With this in mind, I soon felt more relaxed with the process and the learning actually began to progress more quickly.

After about 1 to 2 years of this daily study and recitation, I began to recite the Shurangama Mantra from memory without needing to use the book. Attending the recitation sessions at the monastery and listening to others recite during other occasions also helped to reinforce the learning process. Sometimes at the monastery I would be frustrated that the Dharma Masters were reciting so quickly that it was difficult to keep up with. Eventually, I realized that the recitation actually flows more naturally and is easier to keep in cadence at a quicker pace as the conscious mind seems to gets in the way of slower recitation.

In the current age, there are many daily occurrences that can easily distract us from our own true nature and keep the six sense organs busy chasing after and attaching to things. Although we practice good deeds, our inherent wisdom can seem to slip farther and farther away. It is at this time that cultivation of the Shurangama Sutra and Shurangama Mantra can really help us to return to the true nature that is inherent in all beings. The Shurangama Mantra was originally spoken to aid Ananda at the time when he was dangerously close to transgressing his precepts. I hope that studying the Shurangama Sutra and reciting the Shurangama Mantra can come to the aid of all beings and help us advance in our cultivation as we face the dangers of the Dharma Ending age.

Bow to the Great Bright Buddha at the crown--

The Shurnagama, foremost of
all Tathagatas' practices.

If one can, with a sincere heart,
maintain and recite it,

One can perfectly obtain all that is sought.

PART THREE - QUEH

Q: A certain Dharma Master told his disciples not to recite the Shurangama Mantra and the Great Compassion Mantra because reciting them will frighten the heavenly demons and heretics, which goes against the idea of compassion. This Dharma Master also told his disciples and followers not to use or read any sutra because it is unnecessary. He says it is enough to focus on chanting Amitabha Buddha's name.

A: If people who recite mantras are indeed being uncompassionate, then the Buddha would not have spoken the Shurangama Mantra and the Great Compassion Mantra, lest his disciples' compassion would diminish.

Q: A certain Dharma Master said that when pregnant women recite the Shurangama Mantra, they will have miscarriages. Is this believable?

A: Nonsense.

Q: Someone said that it is best to recite the Shurangama Mantra before 5 a.m. Is it so?

A: As long as you recite the mantra, anytime is 5 o'clock in the morning.

Q: Venerable Master, how come I experience headaches, dizzy spells, shakes and chills in my body when I recite the Great Compassion Mantra or Shurangama Mantra?

A: With demons in your hearts, the Great Compassion Mantra is no longer effective.

Q: Some people say that we can only recite the Shurangama Mantra before 7 a.m. Is it okay to recite it after 7 a.m.?
A: I do not know what time it is in America when it is 7 a.m. in Asia. What should we do about the fact that 7 a.m. in the United States is different from 7 a.m. in Taiwan?

Q: Why do scholars claims that the Shurangama Sutra is inauthentic?
A: It is because what this Sutra says is too real. It describes people's problems so thoroughly that demons and ghosts have nowhere to hide. They become completely exposed. They have to say that the Shurangama Sutra is fabricated. If they were to say that it is real, then first of all, that would be problematic for them, since they cannot do what it says. They are not able to observe the four clear instructions on purity and cultivate as described in the 25 perfect penetrations section.

Q: Proper Dharma exists when we protect the Shurangama Sutra and recite the Shurangama Mantra. How many times should I recite this mantra?
A: As many times as you would like.

Q: What are the effects of the Shurangama Mantra?
A: It uncovers wisdom. To make the Buddhadharma thrive, study the Shurangama Sutra first. To do battle with King Yama, recite the Shurangama Mantra first.

Q: How do we become free of outflows?
A: Go back and read the Shurangama Sutra more often.

Q: Many people say that the Shurangama Mantra has tremendous power to harm. Is it compassionate to use the Shurangama Mantra to heal the sick?
A: Mantras are solutions that do not kill. How can one uphold mantras without compassion?

Q: Is it okay that we use one of the lines in the Shurangama Mantra to cure illnesses?
A: Some people cannot. They may even invite problems.

Q: What method can we use to concentrate on reciting one line of a mantra? How many times should we recite that line of the mantra?
A: Why recite just one line?
Comment: For example, "tu xi fa" or...
A: You do not just recite this line. You should recite section

by section. You cannot just recite one line. This line is connected to the lines before and after it, so to recite only one line does not work. Each line has its meaning and it is connected to what comes before and after it, forming little sections. If you really want to study the Shurangama Mantra, you have to study the layers and know which line belongs to which section before you are considered to have understood it.

Q: The Master said the line "sa dan duo bo dan la" can make us understand our minds and see our inherent nature, and tame demons and externalists. But we have to know how to use it. How exactly do we use it?

A: It is like martial arts. We must know the movements before we use a knife or whirl a spear at an enemy. Just because we have seen a few Shaolin moves and think highly of them does not mean we will be able to conquer anyone we meet, especially since we have not studied them at all. How could we claim that we know just because we have watched a few moves? We have no foundation! The Shurangama Mantra is the same way. How could we use it when we have never recited it?

Q: How can we tell the difference between proper and evil paths, heretics, demons and ghosts?

A: Study the Shurangama Sutra and recite the Shurangama

Mantra. The Shurangama Sutra is a mirror that reflects monsters, heretics, demons and ghost so they have no place to hide. Being able to recite the Shurangama Mantra, we can tame heretics and demons. It is very lucky of us to have encountered the Shurangama Sutra and mantra.

Q: If those who are possessed recite the Shurangama Mantra, will the demons leave them?
A: If they can recite the Shurangama Mantra, every demon will go away, but they must recite it in a concentrated manner. If you do so without false thoughts or greed, then any demon will stay far away.

Q: How do we use mantras to deal with ghosts and goblins?
A: Some cults or monsters and ghosts have ways to give us a headache, toothache, discomfort in the eye or make us immobile, dizzy, insane or cause us to speak senselessly. By reciting this mantra, we can dispel their tricks, rendering them ineffective. I am not telling you to tackle ghosts and goblins for no good reason. If they were on your mind all the time, then you would attract them even if there were none around. You are issuing invitations from your head: oh, ghosts and goblins, come quick! I have a mantra with which I can tackle you! You are being contradictory.

If we understand the Shurangama Mantra, we would, in the

face of problems, be able to dismantle any ploy with it. This does not mean we go around dispelling spells every day. There are not so many ghosts and goblins that we need to do that every day. No matter what kind of ghost or goblin though, when faced with this mantra, its energy disbands and it becomes useless, so it runs away. All this began with our having invited the ghosts and goblins.

This is a mantra of the mind, which means that we have to have a mantra on our mind. Our mind must be clean and free of everything so that its effect comes naturally and as we need it. Reciting mantras is not for subduing ghosts and goblins. Upholding the Great Compassion Mantra, for example, is something we must do constantly. Eventually we recite it without reciting it. The power from the mantra naturally will protect us. If we cultivate our daily practice well, when a situation arrives, whether we recite or not at that time, we will still get a response and the problem will be solved quite naturally.

Index

S

T

V

Verse in Expression of Faith from Dhyana Master Hsu Yun

Proclaiming [Hsuan] Wei's wonderful meaning,
Causes the sect's teaching to be echoed far and wide.
The transformations [Hua] inherited from Ling Peak
Exalt the Dharma Path.
Taking Across [Du] the forty-sixth,
The mind seal is transmitted.
The wheel [Lun] revolves unceasingly,
Rescuing the suffering hordes.

"Year of the Buddha" 2983, the year Bingshen
Written by De Qing Hsu Yun, the eighth generation of the Wei Yang,
at the Dharma Lecture Hall of Zhenru Chan Monastery

155

The Founder of Dharma Realm Buddhist Association
A Biographical Sketch of
The Venerable Master Hsuan Hua

The Venerable Master Hsuan Hua was also known as An Tse and To Lun. The name Hsuan Hua was bestowed upon him after he received the transmission of the Wei Yang Lineage of the Chan School from Venerable Elder Hsu Yun. Venerable Master Hua was born in Manchuria in 1918. He left the home life at the age of nineteen. After the death of his mother, he lived in a tiny thatched hut by her graveside for three years, as an act of filial respect. During that time, he practiced meditation and studied the Buddha's teachings. Among his many practices were eating only once a day at midday and never lying down to sleep.

He cultivated various practices of purity and traveled to study with various eminent and virtuous monks, such as the Venerable Elder Hsu Yun. In 1948 the Master arrived in Hong Kong, where he founded the Buddhist Lecture Hall and other monasteries. In 1962 he brought the Proper Dharma to America and the West, where he lectured extensively on the major works of the Mahayana Buddhist canon. Delivering more than ten thousand lectures, he was the first person to establish the Triple Jewel in the United States. Over the years, the Master established the Dharma Realm Buddhist Association (DRBA) and its numerous affiliated monasteries and centers. He taught both Western and Asian disciples to apply the Dharma in daily life. He also taught disciples to translate the canon and set up educational institutions, and he guided the Sangha members in DRBA monasteries to truly practice and uphold the Buddhadharma.

The Master passed into stillness on June 7, 1995, in Los Angeles, U.S.A., causing many people throughout the world to mourn the sudden setting of the sun of wisdom. Although he has passed on, his lofty example will always be remembered. Throughout his life he worked selflessly and vigorously to benefit the people of the world and all living beings. His wisdom and compassion inspired many to correct their faults and lead wholesome lives. Here we include the Verse of the Mendicant of Chang Bai written by the Venerable Master to serve as a model for all of us to emulate.

**The Mendicant of Chang Bai was simple
and honest in nature.**

He was always eager to help people and benefit others.

**Forgetting himself for the sake of the Dharma,
he was willing to sacrifice his life.**

Bestowing medicines according to people's illnesses,
he offered his own marrow and skin.

His vow was to unite as one with millions of beings.

His practice pervaded space as he gathered
in the myriad potentials,

Without regard for past, future, or present;

With no distinctions of north, south, east, or west.

The Eighteen Great Vow
of the Venerable Master Hua

On the nineteenth of the sixth lunar month, while practicing filial piety by his mother's grave, the Master made the following vows:

I bow before the Buddhas of the ten directions, the Dharma of the Tripitaka, and the holy Sangha of the past and present, praying that they will bear witness: I, disciple Tu Lun, An Tze, resolve not to seek for myself either the blessings of the gods or of humans, or the attainments of the Hearers, Those Enlightened by Conditions, or the Bodhisattvas of the Provisional Vehicle. Instead, I rely on the Supreme Vehicle, and bring forth the resolve for bodhi, vowing that all living beings in the Dharma Realm shall attain anuttara-samyak-sambodhi (Utmost Right and Perfect Enlightenment) at the same time as I.

1. **I vow that I will not attain the Right Enlightenment if there is even one Bodhisattva in the ten directions and the three periods of time to the end of empty space and the Dharma Realm who has not yet become a Buddha.**

2. I vow that I will not attain the Right Enlightenment if there is even one Pratyekabuddha in the ten directions and the three periods of time to the end of empty space and the Dharma Realm who has not yet become a Buddha.

3. I vow that I will not attain the Right Enlightenment if there is even one Hearer in the ten directions and the three periods of time to the end of empty space and the Dharma Realm who has not yet become a Buddha.

4. I vow that I will not attain the Right Enlightenment if there is even one god in the Triple Realm who has not yet become a Buddha.

5. I vow that I will not attain the Right Enlightenment if there is even one human being in the worlds of the ten directions who has not yet become a Buddha.

6. I vow that I will not attain the Right Enlightenment if there is even one asura who has not yet become a Buddha.

7. I vow that I will not attain the Right Enlightenment if there is even one animal who has not yet become a Buddha.

8. I vow that I will not attain the Right Enlightenment if there is even one hungry ghost who has not yet become a Buddha.

9. I vow that I will not attain the Right Enlightenment if there

is even one being in the hells who has not yet become a
Buddha.

10. I vow that I will not attain the Right Enlightenment if
    there is any being in the Triple Realm who has taken
    refuge with me and has not yet become a Buddha, be it a
    god, immortal, human being, or asura, a bird, aquatic
    creature, plant, or animal, a dragon, beast, ghost, or spirit.

11. I vow to bestow upon all beings of the Dharma Realm all
    the blessings and happiness I am destined to receive.

12. I vow to take upon myself all the miseries of all living
    beings of the Dharma Realm, that I alone may endure
    them on their behalf.

13. I vow that my spirit shall enter the hearts of all living
    beings who do not believe in the Buddhadharma, causing
    them to reform their evil conduct and practice the good,
    repent of their errors and start anew, take refuge with the
    Triple Jewel, and ultimately realize Buddhahood.

14. I vow that every living being who has seen my face or even
    heard my name will bring forth the Bodhi resolve and
    quickly realize the Buddha Way.

15. I vow to respectfully observe the Buddha's instructions and
    take only one meal a day and that at noon.

16. I vow to enlighten all sentient beings according to their dispositions.

17. I vow in this very life to attain the Five Eyes and Six Spiritual Powers, and the ability to fly freely.

18. I vow that my vows will all be fulfilled.

I vow to save the numberless living beings.
I vow to eradicate the inexhaustible afflictions.
I vow to study the limitless Dharma-doors.
I vow to realize the supreme Buddha Way.

The Dharma Realm Buddhist Association

The Dharma Realm Buddhist Association (DRBA) was founded
by the Venerable Master Hsuan Hua in the United States of
America in 1959 to bring the genuine teachings of the Buddha
to the entire world. Its goals are to propagate the Proper Dharma,
to translate the Mahayana Buddhist scriptures into the world'
s languages and to promote ethics in and through education.
The members of the association guide themselves with six ideals
established by the Venerable Master which are to refrain from
fighting, greed, seeking, selfishness, pursuing personal advantage,
and lying.

Members of DRBA hold in mind the credo set forth by the
Master:
Freezing, we do not scheme.
Starving, we do not beg.
Dying of poverty, we ask for nothing.
According with conditions, we do not change.
Not changing, we accord with conditions.
We adhere firmly to our three great principles.
We renounce our lives to do the Buddha's work
We take responsibility in molding our own destinies.
We rectify our lives to fulfill our role as members
of the Sangha.
Encountering specific matters, we understand the principles.

Understanding the principles, we apply them in specific matters. We carry on the single pulse of the patriarchs' mind-transmission.

During the five decades since its inception, DRBA has expanded to include international Buddhist centers such as Gold Mountain Monastery, the City of Ten Thousand Buddhas, the City of the Dharma Realm and various other branch facilities were founded. All these facilities operate under the guidance of the Venerable Master and through the auspices of the Dharma Realm Buddhist Association. Following the Buddhas' guidelines, the Sangha members in the DRBA monastic communities maintain the practices of taking only one meal a day and of always wearing their precept sashes. Reciting the Buddha's name, studying the teachings, and practicing meditation, they dwell together in harmony and personally put into practice the Buddha's teachings. In accord with Master Hua's emphasis on translation and education, the Association also sponsors an International Translation Institute, vocational training programs for Sangha and laity, Dharma Realm Buddhist University, and elementary and secondary schools.

The Way-places of this Association are open to sincere individuals of all races, religions, and nationalities. Everyone who is willing to put forth his/her best effort in nurturing humaneness, righteousness, merit and virtue in order to understand the mind and see the nature is welcome to join in the study and practice.

The Eight Guidelines of
The Buddhist Text Translation Society

1. A volunteer must free him/herself from the motives of personal fame and profit.

2. A volunteer must cultivate a respectful and sincere attitude free from arrogance and conceit.

3. A volunteer must refrain from aggrandizing his/her work and denigrating that of others.

4. A volunteer must not establish him/herself as the standard of correctness and suppress the work of others with his or her fault-finding.

5. A volunteer must take the Buddha-mind as his/her own mind.

6. A volunteer must use the wisdom of Dharma-Selecting Vision to determine true principles.

7. A volunteer must request Virtuous Elders in the ten directions to certify his/her translations.

8. A volunteer must endeavor to propagate the teachings by printing Sutras, Shastra texts, and Vinaya texts when the translations are certified as being correct.

法界佛教總會
Dharma Realm Buddhist Association Branches
Home page: http://www.drba.org
Main Branch:
萬佛聖城
The City of Ten Thousand Buddhas
4951 Bodhi Way, Ukiah, CA 95482 U.S.A.
Tel: (707) 462-0939 Fax: (707) 462-0949
E-mail: cttb@drba.org

國際譯經學院
The International Translation Institute
1777 Murchison Drive,
Burlingame, CA 94010-4504 U.S.A.
Tel: (650) 692-5912   Fax: (650) 692-5056

法界宗教研究院
Institute for World Religions
(Berkeley Buddhist Monastery)
2304 McKinley Ave.,
Berkeley, CA 94703 U.S.A.
Tel: (510) 848-3440   Fax: (510) 548-4551

金山聖寺
Gold Mountain Monastery
800 Sacramento Street,
San Francisco, CA 94108 U.S.A.
Tel: (415) 421-6117   Fax: (415) 788-6001

金聖寺
Gold Sage Monastery
11455 Clayton Road,
San Jose, CA 95127 U.S.A.
Tel: (408) 923-7243   Fax: (408) 923-1064

法界聖城
City of the Dharma Realm
1029 West Capitol Ave.,
W. Sacramento, CA 95691 U.S.A.
Tel: (916) 374-8268   Fax: (916) 374-8234

金輪聖寺
Gold Wheel Monastery
235 N. Ave. 58,
Los Angeles, CA 90042 U.S.A.
Tel: (323) 258-6668   Fax: (323) 258-3619

長堤聖寺
Long Beach Monastery
3361 East Ocean Boulevard,
Long Beach, CA 90803 U.S.A.
Tel: (562) 438-8902   Fax: (562) 438-8902

福祿壽聖寺
Blessings, Prosperity & Longevity Monastery
4140 Long Beach Boulevard,
Long Beach, CA 90807 U.S.A.
Tel: (562) 595-4966   Fax: (562) 595-4966

華嚴精舍
Avatamsaka Vihara
9601 Seven Locks Road,
Bethesda, MD 20817-9997
Tel: (301) 469-8300   Fax: (301) 469-8300

金峯聖寺
Gold Summit Monastery
233 First Ave. West,
Seattle, WA 98119 U.S.A.
Tel: (206) 284-6690   Fax: (206) 284-6918

金佛聖寺
Gold Buddha Monastery
248 East 11th Ave.,
Vancouver, B.C., V5T 2C3 Canada
Tel: (604) 709-0248   Fax: (604) 684-3754

華嚴聖寺
Avatamsaka Monastery
1009 Fourth Ave., S.W.
Calgary AB, T2P OK8, Canada
Tel: (403) 234-0644   Fax: (403) 263-0637

美國法界佛教總會駐華辦事處 (法界佛教印經會)
Dharma Realm Buddhist Books Distribution Society
11th Floor, 85 Chung-Hsiao E. Road, sec 6,
Taipei, Taiwan, R.O.C.
Tel: (02) 2786-3022   Fax: (02) 2786-2674

法界聖寺
Dharma Realm Sagely Monastery
20, Tung-hsi Shan-chuang, Hsing-lung Village, Liu-Kuei,
Kaohsiung County, Taiwan, R.O.C.
Tel: (07) 689-3713   Fax: (07) 689-3870

彌陀聖寺
Amitabha Monastery
7 Su-chien-hui, Chih-nan Village, Shou-Feng,
Hualien County, Taiwan, R.O.C.
Tel: (03) 865-1956   Fax: (03) 865-3426

般若觀音聖寺
Prajna Guanyin Sagely Monastery
Batu 5 1/2 Jalan Sungai Besi, Salak Selatan,
57100 Kuala Lumpur, West Malaysia
Tel: (03) 7982-6560   Fax: (03) 7980-1272

法界觀音聖寺
Dharma Realm Guanyin Sagely Monastery
161, Jalan Ampang,
50450 Kuala Lumpur, Malaysia.
Tel: (03) 2164-8055   Fax: (03) 2163-7118

蓮華精舍
Lotus Vihara
136, Jalan Sekolah,
45600 Batang Berjuntai, Selangor, Malaysia
Tel: (03) 3271-9439

馬來西亞法界佛教總會檳城分會
Malaysia Dharma Realm Buddhist Association
Penang Branch
32-32C, Jalan Tan Sri Teh Ewe Lim,
11600 Jelutong, Penang, Malaysia
Tel: (04) 281-7728   Fax: (04) 281-7798

法緣聖寺
Fa Yuan Sagely Monastery
1, Jalan Utama, Taman Serdang Raya,
43300 Seri Kembangan, Selangor, Malaysia
Tel: (03) 8948-5688

觀音聖寺
Guan Yin Sagely Monastery
No. 166A Jalan Temiang,
70200 Seremban, Negeri Sembilan.
Tel/Fax: (06) 761-1988

佛教講堂
Buddhist Lecture Hall
31 Wong Nei Chong Rd., Top Floor,
Happy Valley, Hong Kong
Tel: (852) 2572-7644   Fax: (852) 2572-2850